RETIREMENT INCOME SOURCE

RETIREMENT INCOME SOURCE

THE ULTIMATE GUIDE TO ETERNAL INCOME

DAVID J. SCRANTON

Advantage | Books

Copyright © 2024 by David J. Scranton.

All rights reserved. No part of this book may be used or reproduced in any manner whatsoever without prior written consent of the author, except as provided by the United States of America copyright law.

Published by Advantage Books, Charleston, South Carolina.
An imprint of Advantage Media.

ADVANTAGE is a registered trademark, and the Advantage colophon is a trademark of Advantage Media Group, Inc.

Printed in the United States of America.

10 9 8 7 6 5 4 3 2 1

ISBN: 979-8-89188-093-1 (Paperback)
ISBN: 979-8-89188-094-8 (eBook)

Library of Congress Control Number:2024908588

Cover design by Lance Buckley.
Layout design by Ruthie Wood.

This publication is designed to provide accurate and authoritative information in regard to the subject matter covered. It is sold with the understanding that the publisher is not engaged in rendering legal, accounting, or other professional services. If legal advice or other expert assistance is required, the services of a competent professional person should be sought.

> Advantage Books is an imprint of Advantage Media Group. Advantage Media helps busy entrepreneurs, CEOs, and leaders write and publish a book to grow their business and become the authority in their field. Advantage authors comprise an exclusive community of industry professionals, idea-makers, and thought leaders. For more information go to **advantagemedia.com**.

CONTENTS

DISCLAIMER IX

DEDICATION XI

CHAPTER 1 1
THE INCOME GENERATION

CHAPTER 2 21
SO, WHAT'S THE BIG DEAL
ABOUT INCOME, ANYWAY?

CHAPTER 3 41
A RETIREE'S BEST FRIEND

CHAPTER 4 55
THE PROBLEM WITH A "GROWTH-
ONLY" APPROACH IN OR
NEAR RETIREMENT

CHAPTER 5 73
THE CHALLENGE WITH
TODAY'S MARKET

CHAPTER 6 87
ADDICTED TO GROWTH

CHAPTER 7 99
WHY DOESN'T MY "ADVISOR"
TALK LIKE THIS?

CHAPTER 8 117
HAVE YOU OUTGROWN YOUR
CURRENT ADVISOR?

CHAPTER 9 145
OUR BIG FAT HAIRY
AUDACIOUS GOAL

AUTHOR BIO 155

NOTES 157

DISCLAIMER

David Scranton is the founder and majority owner of Sound Income Group, the holding company for Sound Income Strategies, Advisors' Academy, and Retirement Income Source. The information presented by the author and the publisher is for information and educational purposes only. It should not be considered specific investment advice, does not take into consideration your specific situation, and does not intend to make an offer or solicitation for the sale or purchase of any securities investment strategies. Additionally, no legal or tax advice is being offered. If legal or tax advice is needed, a qualified professional should be engaged. Investments involve risk and are not guaranteed. This book contains information that might be dated and is intended only to educate and entertain. Any links or websites referred to are for informational purposes only. Websites not associated with the author are unaffiliated sources of information, and the author takes no responsibility for the accuracy of the information provided by these websites. Be sure to consult with a qualified financial advisor and a tax professional before implementing any strategy discussed herein.

DEDICATION

Since 1999, I have devoted myself to educating everyday investors about the dangers of certain so-called investment "rules" and concepts when it comes to their retirement.

This is my third book by a major publisher, and, for the most part, exercising my newfound national voice, whether in print or in person, is not a job I initially wanted. I wanted "someone" to build a national foundation of education and financial solutions; I wanted "someone" to talk about the history of Wall Street and to help educate investors about the dangers of what I call "growth-only" strategies versus strategies geared toward income. (To be clear many growth strategies do generate some incidental income in the form of dividends. Throughout this book I am taking literary license by referring to them as "growth-only.") So, yes, I wanted "someone" to do all this, but I didn't necessarily want it to be me.

After many years in the role, however, I have come to embrace it, and I am grateful to those who have helped me along the way.

I have specialists in their field that continue to help me execute my vision, and I truly would not be where I am without them. But my secret weapon of sorts is a group of financial advisors who have been with me since the very beginning. They are the closest thing to siblings that an only child like me will ever have. This book is dedicated to all of them because it truly is as much theirs as it is mine. They are the ones who planted the seed for all we've achieved by asking: "If not you, if not us, then who?"

So, to all these advisors, I say thank you for making my life's work a source of constant inspiration and learning. Together, we are well on our way to achieving our goal of helping retirees and pre-retirees understand the strategic value of shifting their investment focus to an income-first approach.

I also want to dedicate this book to the baby boomers and investors over 50—what I call the Income Generation. I, myself, am part of this group. Together, let's show the world that we are the first generation that really understands that retirement can be the culmination of a great life, that it should be prepared for with the utmost care and confidence, and that the key to achieving those goals lies in working with a fiduciary financial advisor who specializes in retirement income.

CHAPTER 1

THE INCOME GENERATION

If you do a Google[1] search for the word "income," it will generate 974 million results in about 0.62 seconds. And yet, for all the information about income out there, most people still have no idea what it means or how to get it.

I'm talking, of course, about a certain kind of income. Not the kind you receive, as Merriam-Webster defines it, in exchange for some form of labor or capital. I'm talking about retirement income, the sort of money that comes in the door with little to no "work" on your part, since the whole idea of retirement is to stop working, or at least be able to have the option if you wish.

Investing for income is still a relatively niche field in the financial industry. When you consider the vast number of brokers, financial advisors, and investment firms that specialize in "growth-only" strategies, and the far fewer who specialize in income, it's like holding up a penny against a dollar bill. (To be clear, a lot of growth strategies do generate some incidental income in the form of dividends. Throughout this book, I am taking literary license by referring to them as "growth only." And when I say "incidental income," I mean a dividend return of 2 percent or less as opposed to 4 percent or more, which is what you can get with an income-based strategy.)

As one of the few financial advisors who have spent the last twenty years focusing on the world of bonds and other income-producing investments, I know why income is such a small niche in our industry, but it still troubles me. At the end of the day, investing for income is generally a more conservative way to get a return on your investment. Given the sheer number of folks entering or approaching retirement age today, and the sheer amount of money still allocated to growth stocks and other risk-on investments, we may be standing on the edge of a precipice. If the market were to suddenly take another deep, prolonged downturn like those that occurred following the dot-com crash in 2000 and the financial crisis in 2008,[2] the millions of Americans at or near retirement age might not have a long enough time horizon to recover. It's like playing with fire. You're going to get burned.

Unfortunately, most folks who are at or near retirement age haven't received the proper education, nor have the right resources at their disposal, to invest their dollars the right way. They haven't been told or shown how to invest their money in the abundance of more conservative, income-producing investments available to them.

That's one reason I created Retirement Income Source: to make these sorts of investments available to anyone who wants them. Because the fact of the matter is, millions of Americans need these types of investments available to them since they're safer and because they can generate consistent interest and dividends. But sadly, the average financial advisor has no idea where to look or how to find them.

MORE INCOME, LESS RISK

I've watched the world take some pretty crazy turns during my career as a financial advisor. From the financial mania of the 1990s to the two meltdowns in the 2000s, I've seen peaks of maximum greed and bottoms of peak fear. What troubles me the most as an advisor with thousands of clients I've served over the years is that there's still a great deal of confusion about how people who are at or near retirement need to approach allocating their life savings.

On some level, I think most people understand they're supposed to de-risk as they age. Does that mean switching to a 60-40 bond/stock portfolio where the majority, 60 percent, is in bonds and other income-producing investments, with the rest still in stocks? Does it mean settling for low-yielding Treasury bonds? Most people who are at or near retirement, the types of people who need to make these sorts of decisions, have no idea. As I'll discuss later on in this book, most advisors don't either.

Most people who are approaching retirement today were brought up in the glorious days of the 1980s and 1990s bull market when the stock market grew more than ten times its size. The Dow soared from 884 in 1982 to nearly 11,000 at its peak in the year 2000.[3] At that time, baby boomers, or what I like to call "the Income Generation"[4] who were born during the years between 1946 and 1964, were between the ages of thirty-six and fifty-four. Some were approaching retirement age, but most were still firmly in their earnings years where retirement was still a long way off. Even the oldest members of the Income Generation still had eleven years before they started retiring at age sixty-five. There was time to recover.

So, while a 50 percent market crash between 2000 and 2003 hurt badly, it wasn't the end of the world. But then the unthinkable happened. The market recovered in 2007, only to crash by more than 50 percent.

I suppose I don't have to remind you how painful this was, but most people whose careers began in that glorious bull market of the 1980s and 1990s had no idea this sort of thing was even possible. The financial industry as a whole had come to believe that average annual returns of 15 percent were the new norm. And yet, after nearly twenty years of gargantuan growth, it wasn't until the year 2013 that the stock market finally achieved a new high.

That's thirteen long years of zero net growth. By this point, members of the Income Generation were now between the ages of forty-nine and sixty-seven. Many were now entering retirement age, while the rest were approaching it—and the luxury of time to recover from another major drop (were it to occur) was now gone or nearly gone.

Fortunately, there is a better way. You can reallocate your dollars to the world of income-generating investments. That way, should the market have another prolonged drop, you probably won't be forced to postpone retirement, come out of retirement, or alter your lifestyle in any significant way.

YOU CAN'T TIME THE MARKET, BUT . . .

There are lots of people out there who like to say it's impossible to time the market, which is really just an idea Wall Street likes to convince you to constantly leave your money in "growth-only" strategies. If you're constantly pulling your money in and out of the market, you might miss the bad years, but you might miss the good years, too. That's why the conventional wisdom that you can't time the market is true, but only to a point.

I made a major switch in my career back in 1999: I switched from a growth-focused model to an income-focused one. I knew that average annual returns of 15 percent weren't sustainable, so I pulled most of my clients' money out of the market near the top. To be sure, I was met with a little resistance, but as the market started to crash in 2000, my clients quickly realized I was onto something.

A similar thing happened in October 2007, when I warned my clients in our monthly newsletter that another crash was likely, and that this time the Federal Reserve[5] would likely try new, untested tactics to stop the market from crashing to an absolute low. While I didn't know it at the time, the market quite literally peaked that month, and sure enough, quantitative easing and zero percent interest rates became the theme over the next decade. This unprecedented level of Fed manipulation made it more difficult to foresee market crashes.

With that kind of track record, some might call me a visionary, even psychic. I'm not. What I am, fundamentally, is a math guy. In fact, mathematics was my major in college. I told my guidance counselor that I wanted whatever field of study where I'd never have to write a paper. Funny now that I'm writing my third book!

But I am also a student of history. And even recent history reminds us that the market can crash at any moment and when we least expect it, potentially robbing us of half our money and, even worse, robbing us of time. The older we get, the less time we have to recover from a market crash if we still want to retire.

If you're already retired and still have your money invested mostly or entirely for growth, you're even more at risk. You might be forced to "un-retire" and go back to work. Unfortunately, there are many people today who run these very risks. That's why today's generation of retirees and near-retirees needs a paradigm shift to start thinking about this situation differently. And that's why I have my own name for this generation: "The Income Generation." We don't need mutual funds and capital gains as much as we need income.

THE UNTOLD TRUTH ABOUT RETIREMENT

In 1941, *LIFE magazine*[6] was the first to note the emergence of a growing "baby boom," as older couples who might otherwise have had children during the Great Depression at long last felt financially prepared to make the plunge into child-rearing.

However, we didn't define our generation until nearly a quarter century later, when, in 1963, newspapers began warning of a tidal wave of college enrollment as the first "baby boomers" were reaching college admissions age. It's time we start thinking about our generation a bit differently.

We're way past college and many of us are winding down our careers. That's why I have a different name for our generation due to the financial challenges we face as this massive wave of seventy-six million people marches deeper and deeper into its retirement years. We are "The Income Generation" for one simple reason—our generation needs retirement income, because it's a safer, more consistent way to get investment return. Unfortunately, most of our generation isn't getting it yet.

It's not hard to understand why this is the case. The idea of retirement is a relatively new one. It's not that people only recently decided they didn't want to work all their lives. It's that people are just living longer.

Life Expectancy in the United States, 1860-2020

In the Middle Ages, people were lucky to reach the age of forty. After the Industrial Revolution,[7] human life spans took off. And over the past century, life spans have essentially doubled. The idea of retirement, while it dates back to the late eighteenth century, didn't start popping up until the late nineteenth and early twentieth centuries, or just over one hundred years ago.

Anytime you hear the phrase "there are only two kinds of people in the world," it's usually the start of a bad joke. However, for thousands of years, that truly was the case. Prior to the mid-nineteenth century, we had the haves and the have-nots. There was no middle class to speak of. There was no one who needed to "retire." The idea hadn't been invented yet!

That all changed with the Industrial Revolution. With the expansion of industry and our economy, we began to see the birth of a third kind—the middle class, which has come to define all the hallmarks of the modern era, namely democracy, innovation, and capitalism.

It's important to put these sorts of things into perspective because they are a big reason for the issues we are facing today. It hasn't been that long in the course of human history that we've had extended life spans, a middle class, and all these other trademarks of modernity that have made the idea of retirement not only necessary but possible. So, it should be no surprise that, as a society, we're still figuring out what retirement really means, and, more importantly, how one should go about it.

Here, in short, is why I'm writing this book: Members of the "Income Generation" need income because it's a safer way of getting return. They need assurance that they won't lose their life savings should another market crash start to unfold, and they need a consistent stream of income coming in every year so they can retire without having to withdraw from their life savings or having to go back to work.

Until now, there have been very limited avenues for members of the Income Generation to get this much-needed income. Most financial advisors are still stuck mentally in the 1980s and 1990s when investing for growth was the only game in town.

More importantly, investing for income requires a kind of experience that most advisors simply don't have. It's not as simple as investing in Treasury bonds or buying a CD. It's a matter of wading into the pool of corporate bonds, preferred stocks, higher dividend common stock, and other income-generating investments that most advisors don't specialize in.

WHY A RETIREMENT INCOME SOURCE

So, why am I calling it a Retirement Income Source? Because I want investors to think of it as THE source for the one thing they will need most when it's time to retire. I believe investing for income should be as easy as walking into a department store, buying what you need, and calling it a day.

Department stores, after all, are one of the greatest symbols of the middle class and the consumer economy. When Macy's[8] opened its first department store in New York's shopping district in 1858, it was especially clear that we had sailed into uncharted waters. The middle class had taken control, and their shopping needs demanded change. For the first time in history, people had a one-stop shop that satisfied all their needs: clothes, furniture, bedding, appliances, and on and on. You name it, Macy's and other department stores such as Hudson's and Marshall Field's[9] provided it. It was the clearest example of the driving force of the middle class. No longer did the elite determine the course of the economy behind closed doors, but society was now catering to the needs of the much larger middle class, and nowhere was that more evident than in the department store.

Today, department stores aren't what they used to be, thanks to discount retailers and, more recently, to the e-commerce boom via online retail giants such as Amazon. But there's no discounting the fact that the department store has been a staple of American life for every generation of the last 150 years. And I think there's some beauty to the idea that you can go to one place and find everything you need.

That's exactly what today's Income Generation needs—not for consumer goods but for income.

YOUR ONE-STOP SHOP

My career began with the idea of a one-stop shop, a financial department store, if you will. I started out at a small, independent financial firm in Hartford, Connecticut, in 1987 that sought to meet every need of a person's financial life in our small town. Our primary focus was life insurance, but as the firm expanded, we branched out into other areas. Eventually we hired a CFA who took control of our clients' investments. We brought on an estate planning attorney to handle our clients' estates. We even took on an accountant to help our clients out with their finances and taxes.

This isn't a revolutionary idea today, but it was ahead of its time. Back then, everything was separate. You had brokers in one office, insurance agents in another down the street, and accountants and tax specialists somewhere else. What my firm did is take all of those separate branches and put them together, a one-stop shop that local citizens could come to, in order to meet all of their financial needs.

I didn't think about it back then, but that one-stop shop over thirty years ago really set the tone for the rest of my career and a mission that I hope will shape the financial life of every American for the better.

Today, we need a different approach when it comes to preparing financially for retirement. Traditional withdrawal plans based on "engineering" income by systematically withdrawing it from principal at a supposed "safe" rate no longer work—if they ever really did. Yet the majority of advisors still tout withdrawal plans, and the majority of Americans still use them.

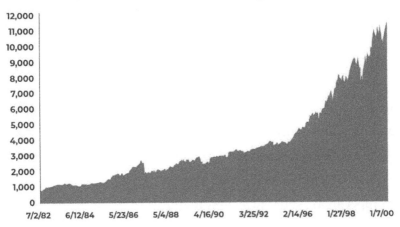

Dow Jones Industrial Average, 1982-2000

Those advisors are, again, still stuck mentally in the 1980s and 1990s, when withdrawal plans were at least more feasible because we were in the midst of the longest bull market in US history. But the game has changed significantly since the turn of the century, which began with the bursting of the dot-com bubble and a market drop of nearly 50 percent that took almost seven years to recover. That recovery didn't last long because then came the financial crisis and another major market drop, this time of almost 60 percent. The recovery this time was slightly faster, but only because the Federal Reserve began pumping the economy with unprecedented levels of artificial stimulus.

The Fed has been artificially manipulating the economy to some degree ever since, applying quick fixes with little regard for long-term consequences. That's why the nearly 40 percent market drop that occurred when the coronavirus pandemic hit in 2020 lasted only months instead of years; the Fed revived Wall Street with artificial stimulus, even though economic recovery from COVID-19 was still a long way off. In a way, this has become standard operating procedure not only for our Fed but for central banks all over the world. As a result, today's global financial markets are, in many ways, riskier and more uncertain than ever.

For years I have been working to establish a national network of financial advisors that can help the more than seventy-six million baby boomers face the challenges of investing in this new era of heightened volatility and risks in the market, what I call "the age of economic uncertainty."

Fact is, of the more than 200,000 financial advisors at work in the United States, the vast majority of them are not equipped with the proper tools, knowledge, and resources to guide their clients to financial security in this era of increased uncertainty. Most of them got their start in the 1980s and 1990s, during the longest running bull market on record, when investing for growth was the only game in town. They were not trained to understand the challenges that investors and retirees face when the stock market doesn't grow for many years. Those challenges only get harder the closer you get to retirement age. So, for many years, I've been working hard to spread this message and bring more people into the fold.

But in doing so, I've had to face a harsh reality. I realized that I could never hope to take on the financial establishment, and the years of faulty thinking that lie therein, without taking my mission public and building it out on a national scale. That's why I launched Retirement Income Source,[10] a one-stop shop that any American can access to quickly reposition themselves for retirement.

To my knowledge, no one has assumed the mantle to carry this message to the American people, at least not on this large a scale. The idea of investing for income continues to grow steadily as more and more investors "see the light." Yet it is still very much a niche approach to investing. The old growth model still prevails, and unless even more retirees and near-retirees "see the light" and reposition themselves soon, I fear they may never be able to enjoy the retirement they've worked so hard for and deserve.

That's why I've decided to take my message directly to the American people themselves, to you. If financial advisors won't make the leap on their own, my hope is that enough people will demand a change that financial advisors will have no choice but to create a sustainable investment portfolio for their clients.

THE DEFINITION OF INSANITY

I believe Albert Einstein[11] is quoted as saying, "the definition of insanity is doing the same thing over and over again and expecting different results." That standard approach to investing, the "growth-only" model, worked for most of the twenty-year period spanning the 1980s and 1990s. But it's been inconsistent since the year 2000, and the global markets have become increasingly uncertain. Yet the vast majority of the American investing population is still stuck in the same mindset that hasn't worked for the last twenty plus years, simply because it worked in the twenty years before that.

It isn't their fault. The fact of the matter is, most financial advisors were never taught how to invest their clients' money for income, and they're so beholden to Wall Street's interests that they have little choice in the matter. For them, it's always a matter of what pays the mortgage and what puts food on the family table. I'm sure we can all relate. However, it doesn't change the fact that the old way of doing things no longer works.

The more you age and need your money to live on, the more difficult it gets to financially recover from another 50 percent drop that wipes out half your savings. If you're at or near retirement age, the question no longer becomes how much you need "saved up" in order to retire; it is how much interest or dividends you can generate from your savings without having to spend principal.

In other words, how much income do you want? I understand this probably isn't the first time you've heard this, but how many times have you heard this without someone offering a clear, written-out solution? There hasn't been a national initiative in place to help protect the countless men and women who are at or near retirement age today whose savings will most likely be wiped out if the market takes another nosedive. But there is now.

This national initiative is my mission. Through advertising and awareness campaigns, we are illustrating how the average consumer can set a goal for retirement and have an income specialist, who is also a fiduciary, help them set a solid plan all based on income, not on hoping and praying for growth in the stock market just to support retirement.

I'M NO PERMABEAR, BUT . . .

I want to get one thing straight: I'm not anti-stock market. But I do have an income-first, growth-second mindset. I am a man in his fifties who understands, plain as day, that if my investments are not generating enough interest and dividends and I get hit by another elongated 40–50 percent drop in the stock market, my financial life will never be the same.

More importantly, I'm a financial advisor who understands that the very same truth applies to my clients.

If a drop of that magnitude occurs and we haven't taken the right precautions, the fact is you and I will likely not be able to enjoy the same lifestyle in retirement that we plan on enjoying today.

Let me put my life in some context for you. To be clear, I have money. But I'm far from what you would consider "rich." I grew up in the small town of Bristol, Connecticut.[12] Nowadays when everyone hears that, their first thought is ESPN because that's where their headquarters is. I grew up way before ESPN was established. Even today, it's still a small town of some 60,000 people, so you can imagine what it was like growing up there in the 1960s and 1970s.

My parents didn't come from money. They were hardworking, middle-class folks like I'm sure your parents were. My dad worked construction, and my mom did factory work. As their son, I decided it was my prerogative to create a better life for myself than my parents had so I could one day offer a better life to my children in turn. That's why I went into the financial industry. I wanted to learn how money worked. I wanted to learn how to make enough of it that I could work on my terms and someday retire, on my terms.

I've done very well for myself, but I'm by no means "rich." I don't own a huge yacht or some 10,000+ square-foot home, but I do own two very nice waterfront homes, one in Florida and one in Old Saybrook, Connecticut, and I don't like to skimp on dinner. I've worked hard to enjoy the life I have, and I plan to continue.

I sat down before I started writing this book, and I asked myself, "Dave, how much money do you really need to retire?" Now most people think $5 million sounds like a whole lot of money. Yet, if you withdraw the standard 4 percent per year, you are talking about a gross income of $200,000 per year. And, if I gross $200K before tax, it's going to net about $144K after taxes (assuming a 28 percent tax bracket). That's not too bad. But now, let's look at my expenses.

My property taxes on both properties amount to about $50,000, my utilities are $24,000 a year, and my average Visa bill is about $5K a month. So, if you add those figures up: $50K on property taxes, $24K on utilities, and $60K on Visa, that's $134,000, leaving me only $10,000 for everything else, including medical insurance.

So, the point is, I would be forced to change my lifestyle and either skimp on those dinners going forward or I would have to sell one of my homes. I would have to make adjustments even looking at a $5 million retirement.

Now to be clear, I may be overexaggerating certain line items such as property taxes and utilities; I like to be overprepared. But to have literally no spending money from a $5 million retirement shows you how serious this situation is. There is a gap here that might mean 4 percent might not be enough, it might force me to eat into that principal. At that rate, I'd run out of money after a couple of decades if the stock market doesn't keep going up, so I better hope and pray I don't age very well into my seventies and eighties. That's also assuming I don't face a major medical emergency that sets me back tens, if not hundreds, of thousands of dollars in a single year, which, with the way medical costs are skyrocketing, seems entirely likely.

My point is, even if you have a $10 million nest egg, you really have to plan if you want to retire. You have to dot every I and cross every T. The reality is, most Americans won't have anywhere near that much when it comes time to retire. Most folks, who will actually be able to retire, may only have $250,000 or $500,000 in assets. Others might have $1 million or $2 million. Unfortunately, retiring will not be easy for any of them if, and this is a big if, they stick to the same strategies Wall Street has been shoving down their throats for years.

YOU CAN'T SPEND GROWTH BECAUSE YOU CAN'T COUNT ON IT

If you have your money in stocks, you know stocks are anything but consistent. One year they're flat. Another year they're up 20 percent. Another year they're down 50 percent. Every year seems to bring something different.

So let me ask you, do you want your retirement to be subject to the whims of the market's chaos? Are you prepared to make sacrifices on a year when the market's down? Will you have the discipline to take some of your cards off the table when the market's up?

If you don't want to have to work that hard and you want to save yourself the headache, you need to be prepared to do something different. You see, there's another reason why the 4 percent rule (which is explained later in the book more fully) doesn't work. The 4 percent rule assumes that in order to retire, you need to have reached a lump sum. It assumes a specific dollar threshold you need to have met before you can stop punching the clock.

If the goal of retirement is to enjoy it, let me ask you this: Does the idea of withdrawing from a lump sum, hoping it will grow back and watching it disappear year after year, sound like fun to you?

Do you like the idea of starting with $1 million in assets and, partway through your retirement spending it down to $500,000, hoping that the last half of a million will last you the rest of your years? That kind of thinking doesn't appeal to me, nor does it to anyone else for that matter.

When I make money, I like to keep it. Chances are, so do you. That's why retirement isn't about a lump sum. It's about income. There's a reason we don't spend our savings in our younger years. It's because we want the money to be there later in case we really need it. So why do we think it's OK to spend our savings after we've retired?

Is it because we know we could be dead in a few years? If so, isn't that kind of morbid? I have an alternative solution.

If the goal of our working years is to build up a certain-sized portfolio of money, then the goal of our retirement years should be to never let it shrink. You might wonder how that's possible. If the goal of retirement is to quit working, don't the funds for our expenses have to come from somewhere? They do, but they don't have to come out of your principal, your lump sum, your nest egg, your net worth. They don't have to come out of stocks or mutual funds you sell year after year.

It can come solely from the income you generate from your investments.

THE ONLY THING THAT MATTERS

What I'm about to tell you might sound crazy; it doesn't matter how big your nest egg is. The only time it will ever matter is when it comes time to have a bragging match with your neighbor about whose personal assets are bigger, and who cares?

Think about it like this. If you budget your money, you don't think about the money you have sitting in savings, because the whole point about saving is not to touch it. Instead, you think about the money you have coming in the door each month. You think about your income. You think about the income you need to pay those bills. If we go through life knowing we're not supposed to spend our savings, why should that change at age sixty-five when we know we might have a solid twenty-five years left? That's why you can't afford to spend down the money you've worked so hard to save over the years. You need that money to stay around as long as possible so you can continue to collect income by investing that money in carefully selected income-generating investments.

When you spend down your principal, your money only works for you once. But when you can collect income off of it, it works for you year after year after year. That's why the only thing that matters if you're at or near retirement age is NOT how much money you've accumulated, how many stocks you have, or anything like that. It's how much income you can generate from the wealth you've acquired.

In the following chapters of this book, you'll learn in precise detail why income is the ONLY thing you need to concern yourself with at this stage if you are anywhere close to retirement. You'll learn why the average financial advisor is not equipped to help you protect your life savings or safely invest your money. You'll also learn the steps you can take to find someone in your area who specializes in generating income for retirement and what you can do if there isn't someone near you.

You'll discover why our economy hasn't been the same since the turn of the century, and more about why today's global markets are in many ways riskier and more uncertain than ever. Finally, you'll learn all about the work I'm doing to start a grassroots revolution that sweeps the financial landscape, bringing a Retirement Income Source to every American who realizes that, in the face of economic uncertainty, a more conservative, income-based approach to investing is the only way to go forward.

I promise this won't be like every other financial planning book you've read that only offers platitudes and half-baked solutions. If I've done my job, this book will change your life, and for the better.

Strap in. It's going to be eye-opening.

CHAPTER 2

SO, WHAT'S THE BIG DEAL ABOUT INCOME, ANYWAY?

If I were to ask you what the difference is between a sixteen-year-old and a sixty-year-old, you might tell me, "Everything." To be sure, there's no one correct answer. The way I see it, the biggest difference that comes with age is the way we set our goals.

At sixteen, the sky is the limit. Our bodies are powerful, vibrant, and full of energy. We believe we will someday write the next great American novel, discover a cure for an incurable disease, or become an Olympic gold medalist.

Said another way, we're all over the place. Before life teaches us its hard lessons, it's impossible to determine what is really the most important thing to us. When we're young, we have grandiose ideas of taking on the world and pursuing our passions. But we have no specifics. Early in life, our dreams are so amorphous and abstract because we don't know what we really want. As we age, our goals become more focused. After decades of work, all we wish is to be able to fulfill purpose-based goals that are important to us, retire someday, make sure we will never run out of money, keep up with inflation, and, for some, to leave a modest legacy. Sometimes, our purpose becomes even more modest—having family at our side, food on the table, and our finances secure.

It's not about settling. It's a matter of setting more focused goals based on where you are in life. Your investment strategy should obviously follow suit. It should have a specific and defined purpose.

And smart investors are, indeed, purpose-based investors.

PURPOSE VERSUS PERFORMANCE

Purpose-based investors are those who invest with an end goal in mind. Maybe the goal is to buy a new car, renovate a home, leave financial worries behind, or retire and leave the world of hard work behind.

Some, however, are what I refer to as performance-based investors. These are people who are so competitive they strive to get the maximum return possible with almost no regard to their goals and purpose or risk, as if investing were some type of contact sport. It is almost as if maximizing return on investment gives one some sort of bragging rights.

Imagine holding your investment statement up to the neighbor's window to proclaim, "Ha ha, I made more money than you last month." Sounds silly, right? But that's essentially what performance-based investors are all about.

Men in particular tend to be more susceptible to this. It's in our DNA. For countless years, our biological history has programmed us to fight for power. If we're not strong, someone else will come along to overpower us, take our land, our women, and our wealth. We're addicted to our own search for power because power is what makes us survive.

This survival mechanism can misfire, just as our own search for power can sometimes blind us. That's exactly why so many folks are drawn to growth stocks.

Yes, the uphill climb of the stock market is exciting. When you buy a stock and it goes up, you feel like a genius. When it goes the opposite way, you feel defeated, and that can affect more than just your finances.

- Stress
- Depression
- Decreased libido
- Higher blood pressure

That's what's so tricky about investing for growth. Anyone can promise they've found some three-step formula for identifying the market's biggest winners. The fact of the matter is, investing is hard. There's no sure thing when it comes to it. Stocks can rise 20 percent one year and fall 50 percent the next.

Here's the thing. Life shouldn't be about working harder to obtain power, wealth, and security; it's about working smarter to obtain these things. It's not about being the "best." It's about wisdom and strategic thinking, purpose versus performance.

The Bible says God awarded Solomon for being wise. Solomon was by many accounts the richest man in human history. There's something to take from that.

MAXIMUM RETURN, WHAT FOR?

If performance-based individuals are completely honest with me when we first meet and discuss their investment goals, they would tell me their goal is to get maximum return with minimum risk. That's a good start. But it's only a start. It's like saying "I want to be happy" without any clear idea as to what happiness really looks like, or what it takes to get there.

The problem with this, as self-actualized individuals realize, is that money is represented by green pieces of paper with pictures of dead presidents. In other words, money itself does not lead to happiness; it is how we eventually use that money that brings joy, fulfillment, and a sense of purpose to our lives.

The question that I have for performance-based investors—retired or approaching retirement—is, "Maximum return for what eventual use?"

The way I see it, money can only be used in three ways:

1. An eventual lump-sum purchase: A second home, yacht, a luxury vehicle, etc.

2. Retirement income: Money coming in the door so you can stop working.

3. A legacy for others: Money left over after you die so your family doesn't have to work as hard.

So, allow me to ask you, which of the above represents your primary purpose with a majority of your retirement?

The fact is, most people age and don't really want a second home, a yacht, or a new fancy car. Most people don't feel compelled to leave

SO, WHAT'S THE BIG DEAL ABOUT INCOME, ANYWAY?

any significant or lasting legacy in terms of passing on money to future generations. In fact, leaving too much money to your children or grandchildren can create problems for them later in life.

However, everyone needs retirement income to last them until the day they die, unless they plan on working forever.

If you answer this question by choosing number two, you would be in agreement with the vast majority of clients I've sat across from and asked this very question to.

Of course, I'm not staring at you from across a desk asking you to be "real" with me. In your head, you might have answered number one or number three. That's OK if you did. There's no need to be shy; it's just you and me here.

The fact is, some of my clients answered differently. For those who answered something other than number two, I usually ask them what they would do in the following situation:

Let's say you retired from my company and I've got $1 million set aside for you as a retirement benefit and you have two options for how you could take it. Option A is to receive our company stock. Of course, you can't sell it right away because you're an employee; it's restricted stock. But you can collect a 2 percent dividend on it, each and every year. That's $20,000 in income. That's Option A.

Option B is the old type of defined benefit pension plan where I simply pay you $60,000 a year for the rest of your life. You don't get any stock, but no matter what, you get $60,000 a year for the rest of your life. That is your pension.

Which option do you take?

I realize it's hard to turn down $1 million, but you have to realize something. Until you can sell that stock, that money isn't really yours. It's restricted. You can't even list it as an asset on your balance sheet if you go to the bank and get a loan.

25

Sure, you get $20,000 in income. But in some respects, that's the best you'll get with Option A. Essentially, the $1 million lump sum is unusable because if you were to spend it, you'd lose your income. Only the $20K per year income is usable. With Option B, you get $60,000 a year no matter what. The key to how people make this decision is that, in the first scenario, only $20K is usable. With Option B, the entire $60K is usable, year after year . . . big difference.

I present each of my clients with this scenario, and each time, without fail, they say they'd take Option B for $60,000.

This teaches us something valuable. When you are planning for retirement, it really is about income, isn't it? Which would you choose?

ABOUT THAT "PENSION," DAVE . . .

Of course, most pensions are a thing of the past. If you were to retire from your job today and an employer offered Option A for $1 million in restricted stock with a 2 percent dividend or Option B for $60,000 in income for life, you'd be lucky to get either option. This isn't the sort of thing companies really do anymore.

In the postwar era, as industry was expanding, companies had a shortage of workers, and they used pensions as an incentive to bring new workers aboard. Today, the situation is much different. Good jobs are more competitive, and most companies simply aren't as desperate. So, although retirement is all about income, you don't need me to tell you that traditional pensions and Social Security aren't what they used to be.

TRADITIONAL PENSION PLANS

The first retirement program popped up in 1889 when the chancellor of Germany, Otto Von Leopold, Prince of Bismarck,[13] announced that workers who attained the age of seventy would be provided a pension annuity, financed equally by workers and employers, and underwritten by the government. And while the United States started experimenting with pension programs in the late 1880s, it wasn't until the Great Depression that the idea of a "social safety net" became popularized. It remained popular until the 1980s when interest rates in general started to decline. Because of this, employers had to make bigger and bigger deposits into the pension to fund liabilities. That, plus the increasing popularity of mutual funds, gave employers a chance to pass that liability on to employees through self-funded plans such as 401(k)s. Today, if you have traditional pension benefits, consider yourself lucky.

SOCIAL SECURITY

The Social Security Administration was signed into law in 1935. As a sort of funny story, the first person to receive Social Security benefits actually lived to be one hundred years old. Ida May Fuller[14] paid into the Social Security system for three years and received thirty-five years' worth of benefits. But she was an anomaly. Back then, if people even lived to be sixty-five, they might only collect Social Security for a couple of years so they could wind down their affairs before they quickly passed away.

Today, people are living well into their eighties or nineties, but we still retire at the age of sixty-five. As a result, Social Security benefits proportionally aren't what they used to be and many feel like they will not be able to count on them. Additionally, today's retirees need to be sixty-seven to get full benefits.

The challenge presented by traditional income vehicles like pensions and Social Security is what makes Retirement Income Source so important today.

We can't rely on these vehicles the way that we used to. And since there are no sure things with growth stocks, they're not a reliable option for retirees, either.

That's why, today, the question is no longer how much money you've saved up; it's not about how big your "number" is, and it's not about performance. The question now is: How much income can the money you've saved up make you, even as it continues to grow?

ANSWER THIS QUESTION

Let me ask you an important question: How does the amount of money you have in the bank, or in the market, affect your day-to-day life?

Really think about your answer to this. If you're reading this book, there's a 99 percent chance you have a modest amount stowed away in a savings or 401(k) plan. There's also a decent chance you rarely or never touch that money, so it's money you're not supposed to spend. It's called "savings" for a reason.

So, besides a lingering thought in the back of your head, the amount of money you're "worth" doesn't affect your day-to-day life much, does it? After all, the money we have stowed away isn't the money we typically spend. We use income for that. What money do you use to pay your bills? Put food on the table? Fund hobbies? Pay for travel? Buy gifts for grandchildren? It's not the money you've accumulated over the years, whether it is in stocks, bonds, or stacked away in a savings account.

It's your income. And that doesn't change in retirement. Unless you want to spend down the money you've accumulated over the years in retirement and leave yourself in a situation where you have less money producing less income, this situation applies to you. So, let's get one thing straight: The amount of wealth you have is only as good as the amount of income it can produce when you enter retirement.

Again, I understand that, for performance-based investors, what I'm saying requires a bit of a paradigm shift. It requires a different style of thinking than they've been taught after years and years of growth-based investing.

During our working years, it makes sense to grow our money, so we have plenty of income to draw from in retirement. But as we approach retirement, continuing to grow our money without considering the income it generates and subjecting ourselves to the risks that come with it is the wrong approach. It's about using the money you've accumulated by a certain point to produce enough income to afford yourself a nice retirement.

RETIRING COSTS MONEY

There's another reason why income is so important in retirement. It's expensive. You adopt a new hobby. You start traveling. You might go out to eat a bit more. And while all these things might keep you young and active, they cost money. Heck, even if your hobby is reading, you still have to spend money to buy books.

Ask yourself, what is your retirement dream? Do you want to have a purpose-based retirement where your life continues to have meaning for yourself and others?

Hopefully, the whole point about retirement is finally giving you a break. It's giving yourself an opportunity to be a young adult again without responsibilities or worries and living life on your terms.

But you need income for it.

Retirement's just plain expensive. It's a luxury, and luxuries cost money. You need to think about it in those terms. This is a crucial point. Most people I work with tend to underestimate just how expensive retirement will really be. But think about it: When you stop working, you not only have less income coming in the door, you have a whole lot more time on your hands. And unless you plan on sitting at home watching TV every day of your retirement, you're going to need income to fill that time with activities that enrich your life!

A US Bureau of Labor Statistics[15] news release in 2022 shows that the average American fifteen years and over watches 2.8 hours of television each day. The average retiree, meanwhile, watches 4.38 hours per day. I can almost assure you those retirees aren't following our business model, because if they did, they wouldn't be sitting at home all day. They'd have the income they need to enjoy their retirement the way they're meant to.

As stated above, your expenses tend to go up when you retire. *Your expenses tend to go up when you retire.* Start getting used to that idea now, because if you accept it early on, you can be better prepared when the time comes. It's not something to be ashamed of, either. You don't have to go into retirement with a humble frame of mind thinking you have to count your pennies.

If you're the type of person who is reading this book, chances are you were the type to cut expenses along the way. You were a good steward of your money. When it came time to buy a new car, and you had the option to buy an expensive car or a more affordable one, you probably chose the more affordable one because it was cheaper

SO, WHAT'S THE BIG DEAL ABOUT INCOME, ANYWAY?

and more practical. You probably took conservative vacations. You probably picked the less expensive house.

The point is, you worked hard for the money you have now. You saved it by making practical decisions along the way. Why skimp on it now? If you made sacrifices along the way to get where you are now, don't you want to enjoy yourself in retirement?

So, let's get two things straight about retirement:

1. It's more expensive than you probably think it is.
2. It isn't worth skimping over. If you worked hard to save your money, you have a duty to yourself to enjoy it.

I've had a lot of people walk into my office who make $120,000 a year and try to convince me they'll only need $3,500 a month in retirement. I ask them, "Are you banking the extra $70 grand each year?" That's when they start to realize they'll probably need more than $3,500.

Bottom line, you don't retire to skimp and save. You retire to enjoy it. To do that, you need a plan. More specifically, you need income.

STAYING SEVEN MOVES AHEAD

So, you know you need income. Through most of your life, you had to sit in an office or show up to work eight hours a day, five times a week in order to earn it. The trick of retirement is to keep that income coming in the door without having to work for it. Easier said than done, right? It's also to keep that income coming in on a consistent basis so you never have to spend the money you worked so hard to save up, unless you choose to (see "lump-sum purchase").[16] The way you do that is simple in theory, but, as you'll discover in this book, a little more difficult to execute.

That's because most financial advisors don't have the right plan.

To set up an ironclad retirement income plan, you need to be able to work with an advisor who can put you in income-generating investments and who understands that your expenses will most likely increase as you age through your retirement years.

Inflation[17] is one of the big reasons why. It is the hypertension of retirement, the silent killer. You have to remember that every year your expenses will typically rise by 2–3 percent or more. That means you have to have enough coming in the door to offset that. If you're using the traditional retirement income model, where you withdraw from your principal every year and have less and less money generating less and less income, it's like being attacked from both sides. Less money coming in the door plus higher expenses is a recipe for disaster.

Most people have a hard time accounting for inflation when they think about retirement. That's because most people, figuratively speaking, are flying at 1,000 feet. At that altitude, you can only see so far ahead, less than 40 miles, in fact.

My job as a financial advisor is to take a 30,000-foot view. At that altitude, one can see over 200 miles, five to six times as far. It is where I can see the rest of a client's life ahead of him and plan it out for him each step of the way.

The average investor can only visualize their life maybe five or ten years ahead, and that's simply not far enough. It is said that the average chess player can only think one or two moves ahead, whereas the grandmaster can think seven moves ahead. It takes a lot of practice games to become a grandmaster. Trouble is, investors only have one shot at retirement. That's why finding the right advisor is so important.

With inflation rising at 2 or 3 percent every year, think of it like this—in thirty years, the dollars you've saved up today may only carry you a third as far as they do today. That means your investment income doesn't just need to be able to meet your living expenses today, it needs to be able to do it thirty years from now.

AHHH, HEALTHCARE

Inflation is just one of many concerns, and a good financial advisor will factor this into the equation, making sure the income you have coming in the door will account for it.

The biggest concern for retirees that almost always makes retirement more expensive than they ever could have imagined is healthcare. I have an aunt and uncle who passed away not too long ago. By many standards, they were rich. They retired in their early fifties, had homes in different parts of the country, including one in Hawaii, went on cruises a couple times a year, and lived a really good lifestyle.

When my uncle finally died in his nineties, he was within six months of running out of money. Why?

Well, it wasn't because they overspent during their healthy years, but because their full-time in-home healthcare had been running them about $150,000–$200,000 per year for years. As bad as it was for them, for us, it will be even worse.

Healthcare costs are subject to some of the greatest inflation rates in the country. The only other things that come close are college tuition and childcare. Since 1948, the price of medical care has grown at an average annual rate of 5.3 percent compared to 3.5 percent for the consumer price index overall.[18] So, at close to 6 percent, healthcare and medical costs are essentially doubling every twelve years. That means if a couple in their sixties is budgeting $200K for annual full-time in-home healthcare today, by the time they're in their late eighties or early nineties, those expenses could be four times as high—as much as $800K a year. And, even if they're projecting an increase based on the standard inflation rate of 3.5 percent, they're still going to fall short.

So, today, if you have $2 million in an IRA, you could afford to have nurses run around and take care of you full-time for ten years. But if your investment allocation is not optimal for generating income, you won't have the full $2 million. Starting at a certain age—which is seventy-three as of this writing—the government is going to make you start taking those pesky required minimum distributions (RMDs), leaving less money left over for later. So, by the time you need in-home healthcare, your IRA balance may be down to $600,000. Combined with healthcare inflation, those ten years you could have afforded today are suddenly down to one or two years by the time you need it the most.

If you've ever had a family member in a nursing home before, I'm probably correct in assuming one of your goals is to never end up in one of those places. I say, if you can't use your money to keep your independence, then what can you use it for? That's a big reason why you want to keep your money for later years when you might actually need it.

Until then, you need to keep your principal intact. You need to use the money you've accumulated to generate income to cover your expenses and to cover forced distributions for as long as possible, knowing somewhere down the line, you might need to tap into your dear old nest egg.

SO, WHAT'S THE BIG DEAL ABOUT INCOME, ANYWAY?

PLAYING THE LONG GAME

Inflation and healthcare are no doubt two of the biggest concerns retirees face, and two of the biggest reasons why a modern retirement plan needs to position your portfolio toward income first and growth second. But there's another side to it.

A lot of retirees make the mistake of thinking they don't need income from their investments because they have some coming in from a pension and Social Security. When you take a 30,000-foot view and look at the expenses you could be facing twenty to thirty years out, you realize you can't afford for your investments to dwindle because of an involuntary withdrawal such as RMDs.

Here's why: Most retirement sources such as traditional pensions simply don't have an inflation hedge or a cost-of-living adjustment. It doesn't matter how much your living expenses change due to inflation. These retirement vehicles will pay the same dollar amount regardless.

Social Security claims to have an inflation hedge, but it doesn't. Not really. One of the biggest scams with Social Security is that, after giving you a cost-of-living adjustment, they increase the cost of Medicare Part B[19] accordingly. The problem with that is, Medicare Part B premiums come out of the Social Security benefit.

Essentially, they write you a check with one hand and take it back with the other. But most people who aren't retired don't know that.

So, you might have some money coming in the door from a pension, if you have it, and Social Security. That's fine, but you need additional income to make up for the fact that these sources don't have an inflation hedge.

Think of your investments as a truck with a towing hitch. No longer does the truck have to pull only itself, it now has to pull itself and the tractor or broken-down vehicle it's towing. If you expect to collect a pension and Social Security, those payouts won't go up just because inflation does.

What this means is that the income you collect from your income investments is doing double duty, it's not just towing itself, but it has to pick up the slack from these other sources that don't have an inflation hedge built in.

This is why you can't afford to spend the money you've saved up over the years. The income you collect on this money already has to work hard enough picking up the slack from these other income streams that don't have an inflation hedge, and if you spend down your principal you'll make it that much harder.

LEGACY

So, if you're a purpose-based investor, and your primary goal is to generate retirement income now or in the near future, here are reasons you need to focus on investing for income instead of leaving yourself depending on growth.

Number one: You worked hard for the money you've saved and you should be able to spend it on your terms. Retirement is something to be enjoyed, and the way you do that is by having your money work for you.

Number two: Inflation means you need to have enough income to keep up with rising prices.

Number three: Healthcare—you can't spend your money down now because you'll need it more at a later time.

That leaves number four, which is legacy.

Many people are motivated by the mere fact that they live in a country where we have the ability to transfer money at our impending death to those that we love and care about. For many of us, that is a very personal decision. And it really doesn't matter what or whom you wish to leave a legacy to. It's only important that you protect your money to the extent that it goes to that person or entity that you designated in your will. Not the government and not Wall Street. The reality is that you didn't work hard all your life just so you could give all your money back to Wall Street because you're using cancerous financial strategies, taking forced distributions from principal, or you got caught up in another fiscal meltdown. You made these sacrifices for a reason. So whether you want to set up a trust fund for your children, give your money to charity, donate to your church, or whatever philanthropic cause you choose, your money can make a difference in someone's life and many will remember and thank you for it.

It really just boils down to this: Do you want to have as much money by the time you're eighty as you do now, or less? If you are taking withdrawals from a growth-based model, there is a good chance you will have less. If you invest for income, and withdraw those mandatory distributions from the income your investments are generating, instead of from your principal, you have a good shot of keeping your money intact well into your golden years when you need it most.

It all depends on what you want in life.

When we were young, we all had big dreams and lofty goals. Then we got a job. Then we got married. Bought a house. Had a child. Had another child. Suddenly, you had a mortgage to pay and four children you had to send off to college, possibly all on one income. We forgot the lofty goals.

After all that, retirement sounds pretty good. If done right, retirement can be more than a dream; it can also be a lot of fun. But to do it right, you need a plan.

OFFENSE AND DEFENSE

There are two phases of the retirement planning process. The first is the accumulation phase when you scramble to make as much money as possible so you can someday retire. The second is the income phase when your planning gets more strategic. Call it the difference between offense and defense.

In the accumulation phase, you're investing for growth. You're heavily invested for growth, pouring money into your 401(k). Since you have time on your side, you're less concerned about the market taking a dive because you know it will allow you to buy more stocks on the cheap and make up for it later. Ninety percent of your investment advisors are perfect for this.

However, once we get into our fifties, we become a little bit more concerned about those potential market crashes. By this point, we've built up a sizable nest egg. Retirement is a spitting distance away. Yes, we could always use more money, but we also realize we're betting with time.

WELCOME TO THE INCOME GENERATION

That's when we begin our switch to investing for income. In the income phase, we're starting to understand it's not just about offense. Defense is important also.

It's the time of our life when we can't afford to lose our money. Sure, retirement may only be five or ten years away. That leaves several years left to accumulate money; this is done mostly during our highest earning years. We can already start to feel "it." Our bodies are already starting to wind down. We're not as young as we used to be, as our doctors painfully remind us. Retirement is coming.

Eventually, work gets tiresome. We want to slow down. We crave a simpler life. By that point, we have to use the resources available to us to continue to survive. Social Security isn't going to cut it, and the pension system, if you even have a pension, is in terminal velocity.

We simply can't rely on entitlements to fund our retirement for us.

That's why we're left with two choices, WITHDRAW money and hope we never run out, or develop a plan that generates INCOME and makes it almost certain that you'll never run out.

CHAPTER 3

A RETIREE'S BEST FRIEND

The idea of retirement is a relatively new one in the course of human history. So, it should come as no surprise that we're still working out the kinks. We need to bear that in mind as we approach the idea of it. There are no hard and fast rules when it comes to retirement. Most of the conventional wisdom is based on a short blip in human history.

That's one reason why retirement planning is so hard.

Because the idea is still so new relative to human history, only a small part of the population is successful in achieving what one might consider a "comfortable" retirement. I'm talking about one where you have little or no drop in income between your last day of work and your first day of retirement, cost of living increases all the way, and little or no chance of running out of money.

The thing is, a lot more people are capable of enjoying a comfortable retirement if they adjust their mindset. For many years, retirement professionals considered the "4 percent rule"[20] to be the magic number for retirement planning. That is to say, starting at the age of sixty-five, you can withdraw 4 percent of your principal once a year and rest easy knowing you'll probably never run out of money. So, according to this "rule," if a retiree has $1 million, he or she can withdraw $40,000 each year "safely," essentially engineering income through these withdrawals.

But it gets trickier the more we age. The government says that starting at age seventy-three you must start taking mandatory distributions from your IRAs[21] and 401(k)s. These distributions start at almost 4 percent and go steadily up from there. By your late seventies, they're already over 5 percent.

So, automatically, the 4 percent rule doesn't work. By the time you reach your late seventies you have to withdraw more, and if you aren't generating income from your investments, you have to withdraw it from your principal.

However, if you could stick with it, the 4 percent rule was considered "safe" through a mathematical model called the "Monte Carlo Analysis."[22] This is a process that examines the universe of historical outcomes over a long period (such as thirty years) based on certain parameters. It produces a weighted-average probability of success. For this exercise, success is traditionally defined as the probability of not running out of money during that thirty-year period. So, if one has $1 or more remaining thirty years later, it is considered a successful outcome.

Some investment companies have actually created marketing pieces using the "Monte Carlo Analysis" touting the results of their "moderate risk" portfolios. These are portfolios that are only partially exposed to stocks, between 60 percent stock and 40 percent bond or vice versa. These results have assumed a 4 percent withdrawal over thirty years and shown an outcome of greater than, get this, an 80 percent chance of success, as if that's a good thing.

In other words, following their model, you have an 80 percent chance of your money living as long as you do, which means there's a 20 percent chance that your money doesn't.

So tell me, if I were the greatest salesman in the world, could I ever convince you to turn your life savings over to me if there were almost a 20 percent chance of running out of money?

Or, think of it this way. In a game of Russian roulette,[23] there's typically only one bullet in a six-bullet chamber. That means you have a 16.67 percent chance of losing your life; you also have an 83.33 percent chance of survival. So it's pretty close to the 80-20 scenario above.

Truth be told, those aren't bad odds. They're actually quite good. If four people make it out and only one person has to bite the bullet, it's certainly not the worst imaginable scenario if you are one of the four people who make it. But it's not funny anymore if you turn out being contestant number five.

THE RIGHT WAY TO CASH OUT YOUR MONEY

When it comes to life and money, the potential reward of a money-making effort is only as good as the potential risk. Unfortunately, a lot of investors today are playing Russian roulette with their money. But it gets worse.

Most Monte Carlo analyses use stock market performance and interest rate assumptions going back many, many decades. This of course, in theory, encompasses good times and bad times alike and therefore is not attempting to be predictive in any way.

More recent studies from reputable sources have published results of similar Monte Carlo analyses showing that a 2.8 percent withdrawal rate over thirty years in a 60/40 or 40/60 portfolio yields a 90 percent chance of success.[24] In other words, an investor with $1 million can now "safely" withdraw only $28,000 a year. And there is still a 10 percent chance of running out of money.

That's why the only way to safely spend money in retirement is to take it from the interest and dividends you collect, not from your principal.

The average person who retires today is expected to live twenty to thirty years into their retirement. If you start chipping away at your principal too early, you leave yourself vulnerable in later years when you have less and less money upon which to draw interest. Think of it like a thirty-year mortgage. Each month our mortgage payments are fixed. That way we know what we're spending each and every month and we can prepare for it financially. But the breakdown of each payment changes the longer we pay it off. At the beginning of our mortgage payments, we mostly pay interest. That's because, each month, we pay 1/12th the interest on the remainder of the mortgage we haven't paid off. If you have a $300,000 mortgage at 4 percent interest, and your fixed payment is $1,100 a month, $1,000 of that first payment goes toward paying interest and only $100 pays down the principal. The next month, your interest payment drops to $999.67 and you pay $100.33 in principal. Eventually, you chip away at it long enough that your fixed payments mostly go toward principal and not interest.

Retirement works the same way, but in reverse.

Imagine paying a mortgage is like slowly filling a hole, whereas your principal in retirement is a pile of money that, as you chip away at it, produces less and less interest, forcing you to take more and more away each month. One month you might only take $100. The next you take $100.33. It starts small, but the problem progressively worsens and, after thirty years, you're out of money.

If you're lucky, maybe you won't live that long, but I find it a little morbid and counterproductive to plan and hope for an early grave.

DOLLAR COST AVERAGING . . . IN REVERSE

If you are invested in growth stocks or in mutual funds, it gets worse. Remember when you first started contributing to an IRA or 401(k) and someone told you that you were doing a great thing because you were dollar cost averaging? By contributing a constant amount of money into mutual funds each pay period, you were able to actually buy more shares when the market was down, essentially lowering your average purchase price.

Let's assume that you were contributing $100 each pay period into a fund. For the first pay period, the average fund price was $10 per share so you purchased ten shares. For the second pay period, the unthinkable happened and the fund dropped to $5 per share and you made your deposit anyway.

The question is: "What was your average cost per share after two pay periods?" If you said $7.50, you are in the vast majority of people whom I query. But the correct answer is $6.66 per share. This is because you bought twice as many shares when the fund price was cheaper and half as many when the fund price was more expensive. Dollar cost averaging[25] helped you "buy low," which of course is the first half of what successful investors always try to do, "buy low and sell high." That's why market corrections can actually be a good thing. When we're younger, we have more time on our hands. It gives us an opportunity to buy assets on the cheap.

It's different when you're retired because you are no longer a net-contributor to the market, but instead, a net-distributor. When you have money in growth stocks or stock funds and the market drops, your money still has to come from somewhere.

The problem, though, is that the math works exactly the same as above, but in reverse. That puts you in a situation where you have to SELL more shares of stocks or mutual funds when the market drops, just the opposite of what successful investors strive to do.

That's called "reverse dollar cost averaging,"[26] and it's one of the most dangerous strategies there is.

When you're reverse dollar cost averaging, your money depletes even faster than in that thirty-year mortgage example above. You end up in a position where you cannibalize your portfolio and leave less of your assets available to draw from later on. Life is filled with zero-sum-game examples where things work great in one direction but not in the other.

It's like trying to put toothpaste back in a tube. It's easy enough to get the toothpaste out, you just squeeze, but if you've ever squeezed too hard and too much comes out, it's a little harder to try to put the toothpaste back in. This is where strategic planning comes in.

THE MOST IMPORTANT EQUATION IN RETIREMENT PLANNING

Commit this equation to memory:

$$\text{TOTAL RETURN} = \text{INCOME} + \text{GROWTH}$$
$$TR = I + G$$

Where Income is represented by interest or dividends, and Growth by capital appreciation.

Let's say that you have $1 million at retirement and that you need $40,000 each year from this sum in order to retire. In essence you are utilizing the withdrawal method and adhering to the 4 percent rule. Also, let's assume that your portfolio is yielding a 2 percent dividend; that means $20,000 a year is coming from the "I." That also means that you will have to achieve at least 2 percent growth or generate $20,000 from the "G" each and every year to be able to get the cash flow you need. Now make no bones about it—you are still taking principal, selling shares on a regular basis. It's just that you're hoping that it'll grow back each year.

Now, I am sure that you don't need me to tell you that, over a twenty- or thirty-year retirement, you will not generate $20,000 in growth each and every year. Some years, the growth will actually turn into a loss. In fact, you can count on it probably two or three times, out of every ten years.

I'm a pilot. Part of getting my license was knowing each emergency procedure backward and forward. I'm expected to have plans A, B, C, and D for virtually anything that can go wrong while I'm in the cockpit.

So, what's your backup plan?

What will you do in the years when your investments fail to generate $20,000 from the "G"?

- Are you willing to go back to work?
- Are you willing to live on less income and sacrifice your retirement goals?
- Are you going to risk drawing from your principal, knowing what you know now? Knowing you could run out of money?

Do you really want to have to think about this and put yourself in that situation?

THE INCOME METHOD

The good news is that you don't have to. The alternative, a far more secure method, is to invest for the "I," not the "G." If you could generate your $40,000 from interest and dividends (and you can), then your principal can stay intact. All of a sudden it doesn't matter if your investments drop in value, as long as the income does not change. No more worrying about plan B or C.

By keeping your principal intact, you increase your options later in life. If you reach your eighties and feel as though inflation is having a greater impact than originally anticipated, perhaps then you can begin drawing down principal. Or, if you find yourself needing in-home healthcare, you might be really grateful that your principal is still there.

As my good friend Patrick Peason[27] says, "If you want retirement to be stress free, invest for the 'I' and not the 'G.'"

I'd rather take all my money from the "I" and leave my principal fully intact for future inflation, medical payments, leaving a legacy to my loved ones, and, most importantly, having peace of mind that I'll never run out of money in retirement.

The American Institute of CPAs[28] conducted a survey and found that 57 percent of financial advisors reported that their clients' top fear was running out of money in retirement. A similar survey asked workers over the age of fifty to rank their top fears, and 60 percent reported being more concerned about running out of money than they were about death.

In other words, we fear financial death more than we fear physical death. Again, it goes back to our earliest paradigm. We made a lot of money in the 1980s and 1990s. For the last two decades, we've fought to hold onto it. Now we're terrified to lose it.

However, there's a better way. You don't have to leave your money invested in a "growth-only" strategy, constantly fretting about another 40 percent drop or worse.

You can invest for the "I" and help to ensure you never run out of money and that your worst fear never becomes a reality.

INVEST LIKE YOU'RE RICH . . . FOR INCOME

It should come as no surprise, but retirement is a lot easier if you have deep pockets.

If you have $5 million and only need $100,000 per year from the "I" to cover your goals, that's just 2 percent. You might just be able to keep a good portion of your invested money in growth stocks. If we incur another major correction, you won't be forced to sell anything at a loss as long as companies don't cut their dividends.

The problem is that most people with that kind of money live a good lifestyle and simply don't wish to live on $100,000. The good news for them is that, at this asset level, they have access to companies or advisors that specialize in the world of the "I." Now they may not invest for the income quite the way we do, but they do a decent job.

This brings us to the real problem. Most average investors, those who really need retirement income, don't have $5 million. They historically haven't had enough assets to access the proper expertise necessary for income investing. That's what the Retirement Income Source is meant to fix. I'm in the business of helping people make what they have work. Many of my clients have less than $1 million, and between that and Social Security, we're able to fund their retirement without ever having to draw from their principal.

TEST YOURSELF: WHAT WOULD YOU DO IN THIS SCENARIO?

Imagine you own a thirty-unit apartment building and you want that building to be the basis of your retirement. You have two choices. First, you could convert it into condos and sell off one unit each and every year to generate cash flow; and second, you could rent the units and live off the income.

If you convert it to condos and sell one off each year, you are essentially hoping that the value of each unit appreciates annually to kind of, sort of, replace the value of the unit sold last year. This may seem to be a good plan for a few years, but as the number of remaining units dwindles, you may find yourself experiencing stress and anxiety. Why? Because after twenty-nine years, you will only have one unit left and that unit has to sell for enough money to last you the rest of your life.

It's not just about waking up after thirty years and suddenly realizing that you've run out of money; it's about the painful process that occurs between now and then. Ten years into retirement, you start to realize that you only have twenty units left but you are in almost as good of shape physically as you were ten years ago. The prospect of living more than thirty years seems to be more of a possibility. So, you start to cut corners financially. Perhaps you take fewer vacations or decide to keep the old jalopy on the road for a few years longer. You find yourself making excuses to your friends as to why you can't go to dinner or to your grandchildren as to why you can't travel to see them more often. You analyze and agonize over every dollar spent. Now, you have been retired for twenty years and are still pretty healthy. But you only have ten units left. So you begin to stress even more as the cycle spirals out of control. It's enough to drive someone crazy, and make no mistake, it does. I've known people, like my uncle, who amassed great fortunes in life and by the time they died they were out of money. It's not a position you want to put yourself in.

That's where the second option comes in: renting all thirty apartment units and living off the rental income. No excuses to friends or grandchildren and no telling your spouse that he or she can't buy something. You can spend each year's rental income with a clear conscience knowing that there will be more next year. Remember when your children were little and too sick to go to gym class? You had to give them a permission slip. Think of this as a permission slip from your advisor to spend 100 percent of this year's rental income and this is where it gets to be fun. Several years ago, I stumbled upon the Barrett-Jackson auto auctions. I was shocked to see how reasonable some of the prices were to buy mint-condition muscle cars from the 1960s and 1970s, the very same muscle cars that many of my male clients wanted back then but couldn't afford to buy.

Most people later in life wouldn't spend the money on a luxury like that even if they could afford it. Why? Because they are programmed to think that they have to purchase it from principal, and, after all, once you spend principal, it's gone forever. Many of my clients who are investing for the "I" are not spending all of their income. I couldn't help but think that, with their excess, many could own that car of their dreams without ever spending a dime of their principal. Without having to touch the principal, it's a lot easier to get a permission slip from your advisor, or your wife for that matter, to buy that muscle car. Or from your husband to do that kitchen renovation you've been talking about.

As my good friend Greg Melia says, "Don't eat the chickens, eat the eggs. That way you will always have more eggs."

If you want an ongoing supply of eggs, you need to think of them as usable and the chicken unusable. Retirement just requires a slight change of thinking if your primary purpose-based goal is income now or later. The income you generate from your principal is your usable wealth. Your principal, the money you actually use to generate your income, is your unusable wealth. That's the money you can't touch; otherwise, you create a slippery slope for yourself where every year you have to draw more and more from your principal until eventually you run out of money. Our corporate airplane carries 301 gallons of fuel—292 gallons are usable and nine are unusable (in the fuel supply lines, etc.). At the end of the day, which one really matters? Do you care how much money you have sitting in principal, knowing you can't spend it? Or do you care about how much money you have coming in the door, your income, the money you actually get to spend?

If you can acknowledge that you'd rather have $60,000 a year in usable wealth rather than $1 million in unusable wealth, it should be an easy decision to make.

If you're not trying to make a big lump-sum purchase, and you're not trying to leave a big legacy, there's only one thing left to do with your money if you're at or near retirement age—invest for income. Go for the "I." We're past the accumulation phase of our lives. It's time to enter the income phase.

And here's the thing: This isn't some newfangled idea. All I'm talking about is getting back to basics.

This is how our parents used to invest their money back in the 1940s, 1950s, 1960s, and 1970s. Back before we had 401(k)s, a multitrillion-dollar stock market, and an addiction to mutual funds, our parents invested their money conservatively and wisely in reliable companies that paid a stable dividend, and in bonds and other bond-like investments that paid an above-average yield. It wasn't until the later part of the past century when we all collectively lost our minds in the financial insanity of the greatest bull market on record.

Now, it's time to sober up.

I can assure you, this stuff isn't rocket science. But to do it right, you need to work with someone who specializes in it. You need someone who specializes in investing for income—not your typical financial advisor.

CHAPTER 4

THE PROBLEM WITH A "GROWTH-ONLY" APPROACH IN OR NEAR RETIREMENT

Investing for growth in the stock market during or even as you approach retirement is a zero-sum game. A stock is bought by an investor who thinks it will go up and it is sold by an investor who thinks it will perform poorly. In the end, for every winner, there will be a loser. The buyer of growth stocks is gambling that someone else will value the company more in the future than you did when you bought it. And the seller is gambling the opposite. Only one will be correct. It's the same with gambling, and similar to gambling, in the investment markets it's Wall Street's casino, where the house always wins.

In the case of the stock market, the average growth-based investor is constantly fighting a losing battle against the big institutional players. The "house" I am referring to is the business that initially received new capital during the public offering as well as the companies (underwriters and such) that assisted in the public offering. That is the "social good" of the stock market, allowing companies to raise capital so they can afford to employ individuals or buy capital equipment from companies that can employ more individuals in return.

The reality, though, is that most stock market investors never participate at all in this function of the market; that is, they participate only in the speculation of whether that stock price will rise or drop after that social good has already been accomplished. For every seller that thinks its price will drop, there is a buyer who thinks it will go up; only one will be correct. Even among the sharpest minds on Wall Street, if you are correct 55 percent of the time, you are doing well, but even then, the house has already won.

When we're young, we can afford to gamble. We have money to lose. More importantly, we have time to lose. But with each passing year, time is increasingly not on our side.

I don't know you. I don't know your exact financial situation. My guess is that, if you're reading this book, you're either at or near retirement age. You're the kind of person who's at an age where it's time to consider reducing your investment risk by switching to an income-first model like the one I've been advocating since 1999.

While I may not know your exact situation, one thing I've learned after working with clients for the past thirty-plus years that is true for everybody is this—nobody above the age of fifty is financially prepared to lose half their money.

Of course, nobody wants to lose half their money at any stage in life. In our twenties, we probably didn't have a lot of money to begin with. The same was true, to a lesser extent, in our thirties and forties as we began accumulating wealth. But after fifty, it's no contest. Why? Because simple math says that if you lose 50 percent, you have to then earn 100 percent just to break even. Think about it: If a dollar drops to 50 cents, that 50 cents has to double to get back to a dollar. Doubling represents a 100 percent gain. During the two times this

THE PROBLEM WITH A "GROWTH-ONLY" APPROACH IN OR NEAR RETIREMENT

has occurred since the turn of the century, it has taken seven and six years, respectively, and no one says that next time it couldn't take ten years. If you lose half your money after age fifty, it's very hard to bounce back. It's nearly impossible.

The truth is that there's only so much your money can grow between ages fifty and sixty. For most, best case means it might double. If you happen to catch a tailwind in the stock market, it makes it that much easier.

But how much are you willing to leave to chance?

What if I told you that it's possible to continue growing your money without subjecting it to the risks that come with investing in a "growth-only" approach?

I realize this is a big paradigm shift for a lot of people. We've grown up thinking growth is the only game in town.

Mutual funds, particularly stock mutual funds, are still one of the most popular investments in America because they hail back to most investors' earliest paradigm. We think back to the 1980s and 1990s when mutual funds were all the rage and did quite well for the average investor.

It's been a very different story since the turn of the century. Consider a study showing that between 2002 and 2017, 92.2 percent of large-cap funds lagged behind a simple S&P 500 Index fund.[29] Said another way, fewer than one out of ten professional money managers beat the market consistently. That same study found that 83.05 percent of these funds actually lag behind the market, meaning more than eight out of every ten money managers fail to match their benchmarks. And yet, most investors are OK with owning mutual funds or ETFs because they remember how great they were over twenty years ago.

57

Make no mistake, it is an addiction. We've been conditioned to think that growth is the only way to get return, that "G" is the only way to get "TR."

We've all had dreams of becoming the masters of our financial destinies, even as we lay beholden to Uncle Sam and Wall Street and so many other forces that work against us.

What I'm saying is that you can still get reasonable returns by focusing on income without having to play Wall Street's game of staying in a "growth-only" approach. But it requires a paradigm shift.

YOU'RE NOT WARREN BUFFETT

There are three things you need to understand if you're going to invest for growth in the stock market. (1) You're gambling. (2) You are often overpaying for stocks. (3) The stock market has tidal cycles, and it's hard to swim against the current.

Number one is going to be an unpopular point, but it's worth mentioning.

If you own growth stocks, I want you to stop thinking of yourself as an "investor." You're not. Technically, you're a speculator.

So, what's the difference?

An investor is someone who puts his money into a business with a plan for making it pay off. A speculator is just along for the ride.

If your plan is to buy shares in stocks that go up, I'll tell you right now, that's not really a plan. It's a wish.

We were brought up to think that if you put your money in the market, it's an investment. And yes, there's a chance it will pay off. But that doesn't make it an investment. I could go to FanDuel[30] and bet on my favorite team and possibly make money. Sure, I won, but

THE PROBLEM WITH A "GROWTH-ONLY" APPROACH IN OR NEAR RETIREMENT

that doesn't mean I invested, I gambled. "Speculation" is just a fancy market term for gambling with one's money to make it sound less like you're throwing it away.

So, if you invest ANY money in "growth-only" stocks, you have to remember one simple truth: Unless you are purchasing a controlling stake in the company that gives you a seat at the table when it comes time for that company to make decisions about the future of its business, you are not actually investing your money. You are speculating.

Warren Buffett is an owner of businesses. He buys controlling stakes in companies. He invests in them in every sense of the word. Us? We're just buying a minority interest and speculating on the board of directors and that the management team in place is going to do a good job.

So, unless you're Warren Buffett,[31] you're not an investor. You're a speculator. You're betting in Wall Street's casino, and remember, the cards are always stacked in their favor. The house has already won.

Let's say I go to FanDuel and bet on a particular football team. Some might say that now my goals are aligned with those of the team's owner, because if the team wins, we both make money. And they might have a point. However, there's a big difference. I may love the team I'm betting on, but the team's owner can decide who the coach is going to be. He might have a say in who plays quarterback and other key positions. He has influence over these decisions, but as a guy betting on FanDuel, I don't. So, although our goals might be aligned, the team owner has some power over whether those goals are achieved. I have none. I'm purely a spectator. So now, take that metaphor and compare it to the average investor versus Warren Buffett. "Well, I'm going to follow Warren Buffett as a stock picker since he's good at picking stocks." Not exactly, because he's not a stock picker. He's an owner of companies, and he's a really good owner of companies.

I've worked with a lot of retail investors over the years. Every single one of them believes that they will not lose when they speculate their money. Every person thinks they have some edge, some secret that will help them get ahead. They've thought of something "no one else has" that almost guarantees they'll make money.

And every one of them is shocked when it doesn't go their way. That's why it is important to understand this. If you put any money in growth, you are speculating. Not investing. That's OK up to a certain age. If you have a job and intend to work for several years, if not decades, you know you have income (there's that word again) coming in the door. That income buys you time so that if you lose any money today, you can always make it back in the future. The equation completely changes when you approach retirement age. Suddenly, you don't have money to lose. You don't have several years of income left to buy you time to recoup any losses you might suffer today.

HOW YOU'RE OVERPAYING FOR STOCKS

I won't win any brownie points here either; all "growth-only" investors and mutual fund buyers are overpaying for stocks without knowing it. Imagine that you and I are buying a business together that is selling for $10 million. I am buying 51 percent and you are buying 49 percent. The question I have for you is, "How much should each of us pay?" If you said that I should pay $5.1 million and you pay $4.9 million, then I want you as my business partner.

Typically, the majority owner, with controlling interest, has to pay a premium for that control; the minority owner gets a discount for lack of control. A typical arm's-length negotiation would end up

THE PROBLEM WITH A "GROWTH-ONLY" APPROACH IN OR NEAR RETIREMENT

with me paying $6–$7 million and you paying $3–$4 million. I am paying almost double for control.

Now apply this same logic to the stock market. Doesn't it make sense that a majority shareholder should have to pay more to control the company, and that minority shareholders should get a discount since their money doesn't get them a seat at the table? Why is it then that when one publicly traded company issues a tender offer to buy a controlling interest in another company, the premium they typically offer to have a successful outcome is only 10 or 20 percent? Not 100 percent? So, consider the two possibilities here. One is that the board of directors of the acquired company is giving the acquiring company a below market deal. The other, and the more likely, is that we, as minority share investors, are overpaying for our minority interest shares every single day that the market is open.

This is one of those things that Wall Street doesn't want you to really think about, because once minority interest investors come to realize they're overpaying for shares, and losing more money than they should when the market tanks, they'll be up in arms.

In many ways, it's a multilevel marketing program. As long as there are new "investors" coming in, and there is more demand for stocks than supply, the program can continue to show returns. And as long as our stock market addiction continues, those prices can continue to hover and levitate.

So, as a buyer of growth stocks, it's important to remember that the cards are stacked against you. It's Wall Street's house, and the house always . . . you get the picture.

That brings us to the third point or problem about investing in the stock market: tidal cycles, or as I like to call them, "market biorhythms."

MARKET BIORHYTHMS

Have you ever asked your broker how long is the "long run"? If you haven't, then allow me to answer that question for you. First, I need to ask you a question.

Do you believe, generally speaking, that history repeats itself more often than not?

Personally, I do believe that history repeats itself, especially when it comes to the stock market. You've probably heard, read, or been told that the stock market traditionally delivers about 9–10 percent average returns over the long, long term. That "average" is actually the sum of two "averages." Over time, 6–7 percent of that long-term average comes from price appreciation; the remainder, 2–3 percent, comes from dividends.[32]

> **9–10 PERCENT TOTAL RETURN =**
> **6–7 PERCENT GROWTH +**
> **2–3 PERCENT DIVIDENDS**

However, those averages can be misleading, especially for that growth component. It doesn't mean you'll get 6–7 percent every year. Some years you'll make a lot more, some years a lot less. And some years you'll lose money.

Think of it this way. Suppose two friends claim they are jogging buddies. They tell you that they average 15 miles a week. But, upon examining their exercise routine, you discover the real story. One of them is an exercise nut who runs 30 miles a week, and the other is a couch potato who prefers watching professional football.

THE PROBLEM WITH A "GROWTH-ONLY" APPROACH IN OR NEAR RETIREMENT

Technically, they still average 15 miles a week between the two of them, but the details paint a very different picture of real performance.

The real story of the stock market is exactly the same.

History tells us that the 6–7 percent long-term growth rate[33] actually comes in clumps. There are long periods of time where the market moves up and down and in the end experiences zero growth, absolutely nothing, zilch, nada, and long periods where the market averages 10–15 percent growth. To use Wall Street's lingo, there were times when the stock market slept like a bear and then ran like a bull. Let me demonstrate by showing you the last one hundred years.

Average 0 Percent Growth	Average 10 to 15 Percent Growth
1899-1921	1921-1929
1929-1954	1954-1966
1966-1982	1982-2000
2000-2013	2013-???

As you can see in Table A, the actual periods on the left were periods of flat net performance. That doesn't mean, for example, that during the 1899–1921 period the stock market declined for twenty-two years straight. There were good years and there were bad years, but history is very clear here. The good years and bad years washed each other out, resulting in zero net growth for twenty-two years.

It's also worth noting that the second greatest bull market of the last century occurred just before the Great Depression, and the greatest one just before the tech bubble.

THE LONGER VIEW

Now, if by some chance you're a statistics nut like me, you may wonder what stock market cycles looked like before 1900. The answer is that they were about the same. We consistently had twenty years or so of bear markets followed by shorter bull markets followed by twenty years or so of bear markets.

Together, history suggests these bull-bear cycles tend to last approximately thirty-five years. Statistically, that means the stock market should outperform all other asset classes over a thirty-five-year period.

If you can survive for thirty-five years without having to sell any shares and you're comfortable sitting through long periods of net inactivity where stocks swing wildly from one direction to the next, you might as well leave it in. If you can't, you should explore an "income-first" approach.

ARE SECULAR BEAR MARKETS GETTING SHORTER?

I just threw a lot of history at you. But history tells us a lot about cycles and trends. What is not discussed enough is the fact that, for many years, the market went nowhere. When the tech bubble[34] burst in the year 2000, the market fell by 50 percent into 2002. The market didn't recover those lost prices until 2007, at which time the market proceeded to drop once again, this time by more than half. And while stocks started to go back up again in 2009, it wasn't until 2013 that the market reached this level again and finally broke through the ceiling.

THE PROBLEM WITH A "GROWTH-ONLY" APPROACH IN OR NEAR RETIREMENT

Think about that. From 2000 to 2013, if you were in the market the whole time and never sold, there was no net growth, and investors who were relying on growth saw zero net return. Could that happen again? Will it? History says yes.

STOCK MARKET PROGNOSTICATORS

Most people don't know this, but Wall Street's main business isn't selling stocks. It's selling optimism. As any salesman can tell you, no one is in the business of selling a particular commodity. Every salesman is trying to pitch you a new idealized version of yourself if you'll just buy what they're selling. In other words, they're in the business of selling dreams.

Wall Street loves to use complicated lingo to overwhelm the average investor. Consequently, I need to explain, clarify, and turn into simple, plain English the concept of Secular versus Cyclical Market Cycles.[35]

When you watch a market analyst on TV, how long does he generally imply a bear market lasts? Two to three years, right? You'll sometimes hear them say less, but rarely is it more. As just mentioned, a full bull-bear cycle tends to last thirty-five years with a twenty-year or so bear market followed by a shorter bull market.

The question becomes: Who is right and who is wrong? Can both of us be right? Do you think there can be different interpretations of the same history? Absolutely. The answer lies in how you define bear markets. Let's look at the 1966–1982 bear market as an illustration.

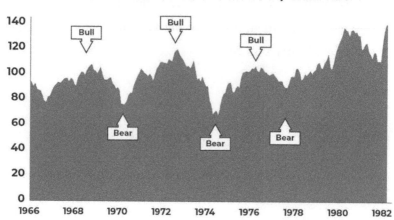

The cycles I labeled on this chart are what your typical analyst would call textbook bear and bull markets. They are often referred to by the industry as "cyclical" or short-term trends. My clients tell me almost daily that, in the real world, when their hard-earned dollars experience zero growth for sixteen years, it's really one big bear-market cycle. So, based upon my real-world definition, a "secular" or long-term bear-market cycle averages fifteen to twenty years[36] or longer within a larger thirty-five-year secular bull-bear cycle.

In other words, within every secular bull or bear market, there are cyclical cycles that go both up and down. For example, another way to think about a cyclical bull market inside of a secular bear market is to imagine a home with central air-conditioning and just one room with a space heater. Sure, the space heater might heat the surrounding area, but if you travel outside that vicinity, the air-conditioning will dominate the overall space.

Given this understanding, why is it that Wall Street prefers to speak in terms of textbook cyclical instead of real-world secular bull and bear markets? As you can probably figure out for yourself, they

THE PROBLEM WITH A "GROWTH-ONLY" APPROACH IN OR NEAR RETIREMENT

would have a hard time getting people to put money in their beloved "growth-only" strategies if they told them a secular bear market was upon us and that it would persist for years with zero net growth.

Simply put, focusing on shorter-term cycles allows Wall Street to speak more optimistically about the market more often. If they can persuade you that bad times will be short-lived, you'll most likely try to power through. But what I'm telling you is that the opposite is really the case. And it does APPEAR that these cycles may be getting shorter, as the rules seem to have changed ever since the Federal Reserve began injecting the economy with massive amounts of artificial stimulus and attempting to manipulate long-term interest rates to keep the economy rolling (which we'll discuss more in chapter 5).

As I noted earlier, the Fed's quick use of stimulus is what made it possible for the stock market to recover in just a few months when it fell by nearly 40 percent in response to the coronavirus pandemic in 2020.[37] Without the Fed's quick fix, would we still be in the COVID-19 crash? No one knows for sure. What we do know is that with seemingly ever-increasing Fed manipulation, markets are becoming more volatile and less predictable. With that in mind, it's important to remember one thing: When you're young, you've got time to weather the storm; as you start getting older, you don't. It's as simple as that.

If time is not on your side, you can't rely on growth stocks. Period. No ifs, ands, or buts. Remember the two major drops from this century took seven and six years to recover, respectively, and there is no law saying that the next couldn't take longer. If you want to retire within the next ten years, or if you are already retired, you need to think very carefully before you adopt a "growth-only" approach. I know what I'm saying might sound radical, extreme, even crazy. Trust me, I was called all three in 1999 when I got my clients out of growth stocks, and I've been called more creative things since.

I realize it goes against the status quo to call investing for growth after a certain age gambling, but that's what it is.

HOW YOU CAN INVEST YOUR MONEY

So, Dave, I get it, you are telling me not to gamble; but are you saying that if I'm not a business owner or a billionaire that I can't be an investor?

Of course not. But when you buy dividend stocks or bonds and bond-like instruments, it's completely different. Let's look at dividend stocks first.

STRATEGIC GROWTH, LESS RISK

When you buy dividend stocks,[38] the companies you're investing in are actually sharing their profits with you in the form of a dividend. That means you're using a strategy much closer to the kind of investing Warren Buffett does. You may not have control of the company's decisions, but they are sharing their profits and, typically, you're investing in mature companies. That's an important point because mature companies hate to reduce dividends. In fact, many have policies to increase dividends over time, thus giving you somewhat of an inflation hedge on your income.

And because these are stocks, they also have growth potential. In fact, one could argue they have more growth potential than actual growth stocks. Most investors, and frankly most financial advisors, are taught that the only way to get more return is to take more risk. And yes,

THE PROBLEM WITH A "GROWTH-ONLY" APPROACH IN OR NEAR RETIREMENT

that is potentially one way to do it. But there is another way, which is by letting the mathematics work for you through strategic reinvestment.

When you reinvest dividends that you don't need for income, you're growing your portfolio with a less risky form of dollar cost averaging. Think about it. With a growth-only stock, when it drops in value, that's 100 percent negative news because all you can do is wait for the market to turn so the value goes up again. At the turn of the century, that may have meant having your portfolio underwater for ten to fifteen years—or even longer.

On the other hand, let's say you were using an income strategy and earning 4 percent dividend during that time. In that instance, over ten years you would have gotten back 40 percent of the stock's value, and in fifteen years you would have recovered 60 percent. But the news gets even better. If you were reinvesting dividends during that time, you were able to buy more shares when the market was down. That means when the market did recover, your account fully recovered much faster, and you ultimately ended up increasing your income. That's how investing for dividends can give you a less risky, more strategic way to dollar cost average. And that's what I mean when I say increasing your return doesn't always have to mean increasing your risk. There is another approach, which is the reinvestment of dividends from high-dividend common stocks.

Here is an analogy to explain this further:

Let's say that you and I had a bet as to how long we could ride our bicycles at 20 mph before we ran out of energy. We could ride side by side and exert the same level of energy. Or if you were smart, you could get behind me and draft off me. Essentially, you'd be saving 30 percent of your energy. And once I started to become tired, you could pull out and pass me.

That's how I like to think about dividend reinvestment in high-dividend common stocks. In other words, you can exert all the energy of taking more risk to get more return, or you could let the mathematics do the drafting and get you more return in a different way. In addition, higher dividend common stocks tend to be much less volatile as a general rule than growth-only stocks. Plus, common stocks typically have a preferred tax rate since dividends are taxed as a capital gain. For medium- or high-income taxpayers, this can be a huge advantage.

Now, I don't want to make this approach sound like a panacea, because no single investment strategy is. But the reality is that whenever you can get more return with less risk, it's a good thing!

Now, let's talk about individual bonds.[39]

INVESTING BY CONTRACT

When you buy a bond, you're definitely investing. Better yet, you're investing by contract. Here's what I mean. When you buy a bond, it typically comes with two sets of guarantees from the issuer, assuming there are no defaults:

1. A fixed rate of interest every year for the life of the bond.
2. A fixed value that will be returned to you, come the maturity of the bond.

There's very little risk involved. You know how much you make. You know how much you get back. It's a contract. There's no funny math, and there's zero guesswork about what will happen. It is what it is.

THE PROBLEM WITH A "GROWTH-ONLY" APPROACH IN OR NEAR RETIREMENT

That's why bonds are probably the single most boring investment on earth. But at a certain age, you want boring. You want guaranteed income. You don't want risk.

An analogy that I always use is that it's like real estate. If you buy properties to collect rent payments, you're investing for the income, and you are also investing by contract. That contract is called a lease agreement. You check your tenant's credit background to minimize any chance he defaults, and if he doesn't, then you know exactly what return in the form of income you will receive.

Now imagine that your tenant signs a ten-year lease with a commitment to buy at the end of the ten years, at a fixed market value. So the income you receive monthly is fixed for the next ten years, as is the sales price at the end of the term. Assuming that you have done a good job on the credit check, hasn't he removed 100 percent of the risk of this transaction? Of course, if you sell the lease agreement to another investor before the ten years, you could take a loss.

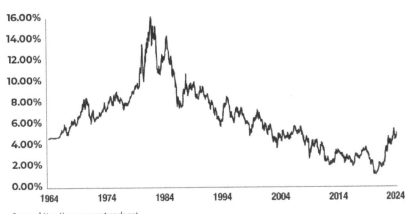

Source: https://www.macrotrends.net

However, if you hold it to term, you know exactly what you will receive. The transaction I just described is very much how a bond works.

WOULD YOU FLIP PROPERTIES FOR RETIREMENT INCOME?

What would make more sense if your goal was to generate retirement income for yourself now, or in the near future? Flipping properties or buying rental property? If you flip properties, you're investing for the growth; moreover, you are speculating. And you really have to do three things well to make that gamble pay off. You've got to buy it at the right time, you have to put money in the right areas and hope it goes up, and then you have to sell at the right time. Clearly it's more speculative than owning rental property where you only have to do ONE thing well—execute a solid contract with a creditworthy tenant.

CHAPTER 5

THE CHALLENGE WITH TODAY'S MARKET

One of the toughest things about investing is that it requires diligence and hard work. Unfortunately, when it comes to making money, most people are looking for a shortcut. It could be something they saw on the news, a stock tip they got from an uncle, or an idea they got in the shower and researched on the computer for an hour.

That's not investing. Heck, it's not even gambling.

Investing at its core is a grind. You get up early, check stocks, follow news, watch the wires, study, research, analyze, and do it again day after day. It reminds me a lot of working out at the gym.

When I was younger, I was big into weightlifting. At an early age I had a healthy respect for people who were bigger, faster, stronger, and smarter than me. I was competitive. I wanted to be just like them.

As a teenager, I started lifting weights at home. My mom would spot me. I started out just lifting the weights we had lying around the house.

I kept at it for a couple of years and started to put on muscle.

Eventually my mom said, "It's time for you to join a gym." So, I did. And I committed to it. I said, if I'm going to do this, I'm going to do it for real. I wanted to be a national champion. I meant it, too.

I went to my first competition when I was sixteen. Frankly, I was too young. Most of the other teens there were either eighteen or nineteen years old. Still, I placed sixth out of thirteen.

I kept at it.

By the time I was nineteen, I wasn't just ready to compete. I was ready to win. And I did win. I went nuts competing and won every contest I entered. I won the teenage overall division, and then I entered the men's division and won in my weight class. There I was, nineteen years old, going up against guys who were twenty-five to thirty years old and beating them.

Then, in 1985, I went all the way. I entered the Heavyweight Division of the Teenage National competition knowing I'd go against the best bodybuilders in the country.

I won.

After that, I quit.

I knew bodybuilding wasn't going to be the career for me. Still, I wanted to see it through to the finish line and see it through I did. I'm glad I did. It taught me some very important lessons I carry with me to this day.

BE WARY OF STEROIDS

Namely, there are no shortcuts in life. Not in weightlifting, not in relationships, not in investing. There is no get-rich-quick scheme.

As a weightlifter, I came across a lot of guys who were experimenting with steroids in the early 1980s. The thing about steroids is that they do allow you to push your body past its normal limits.

But the human body has its limitations for a reason. We now know that some of the long-term side effects of steroids include liver disease, cardiovascular complications, damage to the reproductive organs, and mood imbalance, to name a few.

The point is, steroids aren't natural. When you take them, it's like performing a lab experiment on your body.

Imagine you and I were working out and we came across a guy on steroids benching 400 pounds in the gym. We make a bet. I wager that once he goes back off the steroids he can only bench 300 pounds, and you bet 350.

Here's the thing: We're both speculating. It's a complete gamble how much he'll be able to bench once the steroids go out of his system.

But we know one thing for sure. He probably can't bench the 400 pounds without them. So, why am I telling you all this?

The reason is that following the financial crisis, we embarked upon the greatest financial lab experiment in the history of mankind.

When the market dropped by half between 2000 and 2002, it was the greatest crash our country had experienced since the Great Depression. It was easily the biggest crash in our lifetimes, at the time. Most people didn't know that sort of thing was possible, especially after nearly twenty years of double-digit annual gains in the stock market.

When it happened again in 2007, only worse, it set in a panic, as you well remember. That's why government and central banks around the world resorted to experimental measures to artificially bolster the economy, prop up the stock market, and get the financial system running again. In a very literal sense, they injected the markets with steroids, and they've done it many more times since, most notably and dramatically in response to the market drop that occurred when the coronavirus was declared a pandemic in March of 2020. I'll talk more about that shortly.

FINANCIAL ENGINEERING

Ultimately, there has been a ton of financial engineering at play that has dramatically influenced the markets and economy overall ever since the financial crisis. The first force driving that influence is the Federal Reserve and their use of economic steroids.

I'm sure you're all familiar with this story, so I don't need to beat you over the head with it. Suffice to say, former Federal Reserve chair Ben Bernanke[40] took an unprecedented move when he decided to slash the overnight Fed Funds Rate to zero percent during the heart of the financial crisis in 2008 and 2009. The Fed Funds Rate is the interest rate that banks charge when they lend each other money overnight and it's the interest rate upon which most other interest rates are based. When the Federal Reserve sets interest rate policy, they do it through control of this interest rate. When it falls, most other interest rates fall, and vice versa.

This artificially propped up the economy by encouraging people to borrow money, spend it, and get the economy moving. When you can borrow money at essentially zero percent interest rates, money is practically free, and who doesn't love free stuff?

But that's not all the Federal Reserve did. They also engineered a radical program called quantitative easing,[41] in which they repurchased trillions of dollars' worth of US Treasury bonds.

For those who have heard this term ad nauseam but don't fully understand what it is, it's when a central bank, like the Federal Reserve, introduces new money into the money supply. It's as simple as that, but the way it works is slightly complicated.

Essentially what the Fed started doing was buying a whole bunch of Treasuries from other banks, thereby artificially inflating their demand, driving long-term interest rates downward and injecting a ton of cash into the capital markets.

Where did the Fed get the money to purchase these assets? They simply created it out of thin air. Central banks[42] alone have this unique power.

The idea was that a larger money supply, combined with lower short- and long-term interest rates, would encourage banks to make more loans and, in turn, allow consumers and business owners to take on more debt, refinance their homes, start or expand businesses, and so on. There was just one problem: People, for a long time, weren't dumb enough to take the bait. Homeowners, investors, and the like weren't exactly jumping out of their seats to take on more debt, even at near-zero percent interest rates, because they had just barely survived the worst financial crisis we'd seen in our lifetimes. That's why it took the Federal Reserve three rounds of quantitative easing (four if you count Operation Twist,[43] which, essentially, was quantitative easing under a different brand) to get a modicum of an effect. Between 2008 and 2015, the Fed's balance sheet ballooned from $900 billion to $4.5 trillion. In other words, they bought back $3.6 trillion in debt to get the economy moving from a dead stop to a slow crawl.

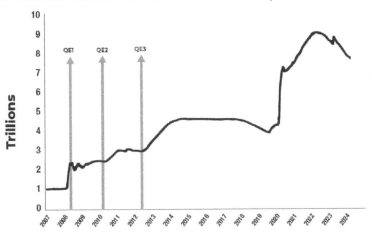

Source: https://www.statista.com

STEROIDS DO HAVE SIDE EFFECTS

So, what did responsible individuals do with the extra money supply if they didn't spend it? They saved or invested it. And with lower interest rates, investors were tempted to move up the risk curve and pour more money into the stock market as other interest-bearing alternatives appeared less attractive.

There's another effect as well. Quantitative easing also puts a ceiling on the value of our currency. This made the stock market more attractive to foreign investors.

The result? A stock market recovery that was much greater than most expected, and a larger-than-ever disparity between economic classes in our country.

Yet, despite these side effects and all the controversy surrounding quantitative easing, a lot of people think it worked—and it did work, depending on how you slice it. After all, we're a lot better off today than we were at the bottom of the financial crisis in 2008. But part of the reason we're better off is that the Fed has not only continued with its liberal use of quantitative easing and interest rate manipulation in recent years, they've upped the ante. As mentioned, the most dramatic example of this can be seen in their response to the coronavirus pandemic. In two emergency meetings in early and mid-March 2020, the Fed dropped its benchmark short-term interest rate back down to near-zero, approved more quantitative easing to the tune of about $1.7 trillion in US Treasury purchases, and created several new temporary lending and funding facilities for business.

The Fed was praised for its response to the pandemic, and one could argue its actions were necessary to save the economy from complete collapse. But the fact that these moves spurred the stock market to full recovery within a few short months, and that the markets were growing again by year's end, illustrates the unnatural and potentially dangerous impact of economic steroids. Even with millions of businesses still closed and the unemployment rate at record highs, by the end of 2020 the Dow gained 6.6 percent, the S&P 500 gained 15.6 percent, and the Nasdaq[44] was up an astonishing 43.7 percent! What's wrong with this picture?

What's wrong is the same thing that has been wrong to varying degrees ever since the Fed started pumping the economy full of steroids following the financial crisis. What's wrong is that it affects market volatility, blurs the lines between what's real versus artificial, and makes "growth-only" investing even more risky than it is under normal circumstances. How long can this disconnect continue without any repercussions?

Who knows, but I don't think anyone in their right mind truly believes you can just create money out of thin air and not have to pay for it later. Eventually, the chickens may come home to roost. As for when and how it might happen, that's the scary question.

QUANTITATIVE EASING ISN'T THE ONLY PROBLEM

But it isn't just the Fed's ongoing reckless use of quantitative easing that has blurred the lines between economic realities and artificial manipulation and made investing for growth riskier and more challenging for everyday investors. There are other forces and factors at play, some of which emerged (like quantitative easing) in the wake of the financial crisis, and others that have developed more recently. Let's discuss a few of them one by one.

RETIREMENT INCOME SOURCE

CORPORATE BUYBACKS

One of the main artificial forces is the corporate buyback. In a buyback, corporations repurchase shares of their own stock to limit the number of shares on the open market, thereby increasing the value of each remaining share. Since the CEO's job is to increase the value of the company's shares for its shareholders, this is one quick and easy tactic that can raise share prices without fundamentally growing the company or reinvesting in the business. It's fine here and there, but it's quite frankly been abused in recent years.

Apple Inc.[45] was the first company to hit the $1 trillion mark, so I'll use them as an example of what this looks like.

Let's say Apple had five billion available shares in the open market. At a $1 trillion valuation, those shares would be worth $200 apiece. But Apple's management and board of directors have a fiduciary duty to their shareholders to increase the value of Apple's stock. Since Apple hasn't come out with many new or original products in quite a while, their share price has been kept afloat by regurgitating the same product over and over until, lo and behold, it no longer works. They also do it through stock buybacks.

Using that example of five billion available shares, let's say they just repurchase one hundred million shares, or 2 percent of the total shares outstanding. That leaves $1 trillion in valuation divided across 4.9 billion remaining shares. Each share is now worth $204.08, or an increase of roughly 2 percent for every shareholder of Apple's stock.

It sounds innocent enough, until you realize that these stock buybacks account for a significant portion of the market's gains since 2008. Since 2010, US corporations have spent over $5.3 trillion buying back their own stock.[46] It has been widely documented that the single biggest buyer of US stocks has been US corporations themselves.

THE CHALLENGE WITH TODAY'S MARKET

This chart illustrates how corporate buybacks move in lockstep with the stock market. Corporations repurchase shares of their own stock to keep the market moving.

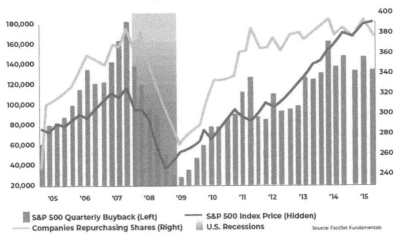

FEWER STOCKS

In addition to buybacks, another issue that makes investing for growth more challenging today is the fact that there are simply fewer stocks to pick from on the open market.

The count of publicly listed companies that trade on US exchanges has fallen significantly from its peak in 1996, when the number exceeded 8,000. Today that count has dropped by more than 50 percent to just 3,700, according to data from the Center for Research in Security Prices, LLC.[47]

Does this mean America has half as many companies as it did thirty years ago? No. Of course not. The main reason there are fewer stocks for sale is that companies are increasingly raising money privately through private equity because it's easier. Staying private also means these companies can remain outside the scrutiny of the public, including regulatory agencies. Publicly listed companies are subject to regulatory oversight and disclosure laws that private companies can avoid.

MORE INDEXING PRODUCTS

Adding to this problem is the fact that, along with fewer companies, there are more indexing products available now containing numerous companies. Index funds,[48] which hardly existed fifty years ago, now play a prominent role in global financial markets. Growth-based financial planners, in particular, use index products extensively because they provide an easy path to diversifying their clients' portfolios, and an easy way to manage the accounts because that task is up to the fund manager—as I discuss elsewhere in this book.

The problem is that stocks within these index products have an element of demand that can tend to be artificial; their demand is greater simply because they're within the fund, while companies outside of these products have less demand by comparison regardless of their merits. So, one could argue stocks within an index fund are artificially manipulated to the upside in much the same way that other aspects of the market are artificially manipulated by stock buybacks and quantitative easing.

RISE OF THE ROBOTS

Another factor blurring the line between what's "real" and what isn't in the markets these days is the rise in computer trading. Algorithmic trading,[49] which relies heavily on programmed instructions, has been on the rise in US and global equity markets since the turn of the century.

As of 2023, it accounted for about 60–73 percent of all equities trading on US markets, about 60 percent in Europe and 45 percent in

THE CHALLENGE WITH TODAY'S MARKET

the Asia-Pacific, according to Select USA.[50] Since algorithmic trades are preprogrammed they happen rapidly and can skew the market in certain ways that can be confusing or ultimately costly to human investors. To a large extent, most of the market volatility we see in any given period today is driven by machines.

LESS INFORMATION, NOT MORE

Yet another factor making the markets more challenging for investors is the decrease in the number of companies out there doing proprietary trading. This is another issue that—like the Fed's overuse of quantitative easing—arose as part of the fallout from the financial crisis in 2008. In response to the crisis, Congress passed the Dodd-Frank Wall Street Reform and Consumer Protection Act,[51] the most far-reaching Wall Street reform bill in history. Commonly known as Dodd-Frank, the bill was signed into law in July 2010.

One of the unintended consequences of Dodd-Frank is that it made it less attractive for big financial firms to do proprietary trading, which, very basically, means trading to make a profit for the firm rather than earn a commission or trade on behalf of clients.

When big firms are investing for themselves, the extensive research they conduct is able to help them on both the sell-side and the buy-side. By extension, other traders and portfolio managers throughout the industry also have access to that helpful research.

But thanks to certain provisions in the Dodd-Frank bill, the big firms today are doing much less proprietary trading, which decreases the amount of research data available to all professional investors.

When you put all the pieces of the puzzle together, what you have is a convoluted picture full of artificial forces that make equity analysis more challenging than ever—thus making growth-only investing riskier than ever.

Here's the full picture: Assuming you participated 100 percent of the time, we had the greatest bull market in US history in the 1980s and 1990s. From 2000 to 2013, the market gained absolutely no ground. Since then, some of the market's gains can be attributed to financial engineering on behalf of our central banks and corporations. The question is, how much?

Whatever the answer may be, this is not the stuff that a secular bull market is made of. It is the sign of an addict refusing to come to terms with their addiction. But what is the next "fix" going to be? How long can the gravy train keep rolling until we run into a wall? No one knows for sure, of course, but I suggest all investors need to keep the cautionary words of Clint Eastwood's Dirty Harry Callahan in mind: "Do you feel lucky?"

THE WHOLE POINT

Once again, what it comes down to is the fact that we are living in a brand-new age of economic uncertainty, one in which many of the old textbook rules and guidelines for investing and retirement planning have become outdated. Adding to that fact is the need for new rules and strategies and the host of financial challenges unique to today's generation of retirees and near-retirees, challenges that our parents and grandparents didn't face. These include the near-disappearance of defined benefit pension plans, the ever-rising cost of healthcare, the fact that many people near retirement age are caring for aging parents and/or grown children, and the reality that life expectancy rates are higher than ever, meaning that people need to prepare for at least thirty years of reliable retirement income.

As noted before, many people are taught that to increase your returns you must increase growth. However, they aren't taught that they can increase returns through an income-first strategy.

So, my point is this: If you don't want to invest in income investments because you've got a $1-million-per-year pension and you're only spending $100K a year, then maybe you invest in the "I" because you want to be a good steward of your money and you want to protect it.

Remember, income is just a component of return. It's an alternative to growth. You don't need to make growth your primary focus. If you do, you might get a 40 percent hit. Alternatively, if you invest for income first, you get a more consistent return.

And that's the whole point. Do you really want to bet there won't ever be another market downturn similar to those we saw from 2000 to 2007 and from 2008 to 2013—especially knowing that the market has been propped up for many years now by trillions of dollars' worth of economic steroids and financial engineering?

Can you really bet that a bull market will be around for the rest of your life and that we won't see another fifteen- to twenty-year bear market? Can you afford, at this point in your life, to take another 40 percent hit? Or do you think you'd be better off settling for a more consistent income goal of 4–5 percent every year with an income-first, growth-second approach, knowing it might actually leave you better off than if you left your money in a "growth-only" approach?

CHAPTER 6

ADDICTED TO GROWTH

There's a story I like to tell my colleagues and clients, a parable, if you will, about a little girl who doesn't understand why her mother cuts the ends off of the roast before she sticks it in the oven. From the daughter's point of view, it seems like wasting a perfectly good slice of meat. "Mom, why do you cut the ends off the roast?" the daughter eventually asks.

The mother replies, "Because, sweetie, that's the way we've always done it. It's the way your grandma did it."

The daughter, unsatisfied, asks, "But why?"

Her mother, with a clear answer, responds, "Well, we're going to grandma's house this weekend. When we get there, you can ask her."

That weekend, they go to grandma's house and the little girl asks, "Grandma, why do we cut the ends off the roast before we put it in the oven?"

The grandma laughs and says, "Oh, honey, I haven't done that in years. I used to do that when your mom was little because back then our roasting pan was so small we had to cut the ends off to make it fit."

This parable illustrates a prescient fact: humans are creatures of habit. We tend to repeat our behavior, even when it defies rational logic and we've forgotten why we do what we do in the first place. It shows how our earliest experiences shape our paradigms, whether or not they make sense.

It's the same when it comes to investing. Our generation's earliest investing experience came in the 1980s and 1990s, during the single greatest bull market in US history.

In 1980, the Dow Jones average closing price was 891. By the year 2000, it had climbed to nearly 11,000.[52] Back then, you couldn't lose money investing in growth. Annual returns of 15–20 percent became the new math. P/E ratios of thirty-plus times that of earnings or more became normal. We rationalized it until it blew up in our faces. But even after two crashes, it doesn't matter, because that was our first paradigm.[53] We've forgotten that total return has two components, the income and the growth, and it's no wonder why.

Our generation was led into the best bull market in US history with the perfect storm: the onset of 401(k)s and the emerging popularity of mutual funds. No longer was the stock market exclusively for the affluent; it had become a place for the average investor. Since investing in individual stocks in 401(k)s required too much research, the popularity of mutual funds skyrocketed. Now, investing in "the market" had become so simple that anyone could do it and anyone did. With more money flowing into the market than ever before, it rose faster, causing investors to speculate even more, and the cycle was off and running.

Fortunately, thanks to the sheer magnitude of that bull run, the average investor did very well, at least for a while. Suddenly, we started to believe that anyone could become rich, that everyone could achieve the American Dream, and with the rise of 401(k)s and the ease of mutual funds, it seemed more than possible.

By the late 1990s, we had become a country of investors addicted to a primarily growth-based strategy in stocks and stock mutual funds. The young lady at the checkout register and the young man stocking shelves would spend their break time debating whether eBay or Amazon.com had more upside potential. TV shows dedicated to the stock market became more and more popular as everyone wanted a piece of that American Dream. Many began to forget that they were speculating, gambling, if you will, and thought they were mini-Warren Buffetts.

Then, beginning in 2000, everything began to change. As we discussed in chapter 3, for the next nearly fourteen years the market was underwater and struggled to get back to even. But that hasn't broken our addiction to investing primarily for growth. The funny thing about addiction, and the behaviors that form from our earliest paradigms, is that we continue to give into our addictions even when they can be bad for you.

HABITS DIE HARD

In 1999, when I was convinced the market was too frothy, I started pulling my clients' money out of the market BEFORE the tech bubble burst. And you better believe me when I say I pulled it out kicking and screaming. These were the end of the so-called "good ol' days" when stocks would double in a day simply by adding the words "dot com" at the end of their name, the days when you'd talk to bellhops and store clerks who were getting "rich" off high-flying tech stocks. People were out of their minds. The party was hot and no one wanted it to end. No one believed it could.

Months later, when the market crashed, I received a small cartful of letters from clients thanking me for quite literally saving their financial lives, after their money had grown exponentially in the bull market and I pulled them out near the top.

Ever since, I've dedicated my financial career to focusing on an income-first, growth-second approach, because I realized you can't always count on the "G." And from what I know of economics, I knew it would be broken for some time—years, if not decades.

Still, there are lots of people who don't want to make the switch. And I understand why. Human beings are creatures of habit. We don't like change. Which is why, when a new client walks in my door and I start talking about radically altering their financial strategy to focus on the "I," I'm often met with a bit of resistance. But it's not because what I'm saying doesn't make sense. It's because they haven't heard it before.

After all, our generation was raised on the glorious days of the 1980s and 1990s bull market when stocks were a sure thing. That's our paradigm. It's our reality.

But investing for income isn't some newfangled concept.

After all, it's what our parents' generation did. Most who retired in the twentieth century had Social Security and some sort of pension. Those with investments owned bonds and dividend stocks. They had income. When the stock market changed the tide in the year 2000 onward, it may have affected them emotionally, but it didn't force them to change their lifestyles, because they still had income.

It's different with our generation.

Those who retired in the last few years are depending more and more on their investments to fulfill basic needs. Without the proper income, many are utilizing the withdrawal method, and are lucky in that they haven't been doing it long enough to risk running out of money yet. Worse, many have "enabled" their growth-addicted portfolios by working longer or making drastic lifestyle changes to temporarily reduce the withdrawals needed, but that can't last forever.

The problem is that the more money you withdraw, the less income you can generate, and the less money you'll have when you actually need it. Then the double whammy—so long as your money is in growth stocks or funds, you risk getting wiped out the next time the market takes a hit. So again, what I'm advocating isn't some new idea, it's actually about implementing the prudence from our parent's generation, so you never risk running out of money. This is about getting back to basics, so you don't have to take those risks I just mentioned. It's about doing what our parents did, and their parents before them, and not letting our culture's addiction to growth allow us to forget a simple truth: When you are at or near retirement, you are gambling with time. You are in the casino, and the years of your life remaining are your chips.

WHY HAS NO ONE EVER TOLD ME THIS?

If this sounds new to you, let's face it, most of us didn't have a lot of money invested in the markets before 1980. That was more than forty years ago. Our generation doesn't know what investing for the "I" looks like. We've only been taught the "G."

But this is where a keen understanding of history helps. Do you remember how many years it takes for a full secular bull-bear cycle to unfold?[54] Nearly thirty-five years. This means that most investors today haven't yet experienced all four seasons of the stock market.

Imagine if you were moving from sunny Florida to frigid Maine in the late spring or early summer. Could you really know what to expect in the winter? Of course not. You haven't experienced all four seasons yet.

In life, don't our earliest experiences in any realm shape our paradigms?

Once again, most investors today were raised during the glorious days of the 1980s and 1990s bull market when stocks rose 15 percent on average every year. The long-term average is roughly 7 percent. That means for almost twenty years, the market was nearly doubling its average annual return.

When the first ten or twenty years of your experience as an investor starts with 15 percent annual growth, you don't forget it. It programs you to expect above-average growth even if, for the next fourteen years, from 2000 to 2013, you received zero. But that's why long-term averages only tell half the story.

OPTIMISM

Back in May of 2009, the University of Kansas and Gallup presented a study at the Association for Psychological Science[55] on whether humans are more optimistic or pessimistic by nature. It was 2009, mind you, and people had just come out of the worst economic hit since the Great Depression and had no idea at that point that the worst was over.

Yet, the study, a sample of 150,000 adults that is representative of approximately 95 percent of the world population, found that the majority, 89 percent, expected the next five years to be as good or better than their current life, and that 95 percent of them expected their life to be as good or better at the end of those five years.

These results show overwhelming evidence that mankind is optimistic by nature. No doubt, there are plenty of benefits to being optimistic. Imagine the cancer patient that loses the battle but remains hopeful until the very end. The sports fan who enters every season thinking his team will win the championship this year even though they've never come close. The lottery ticket buyer who has bought 1,000 Lottos and still remains hopeful. The stock speculator who lost money on his last dozen trades but is going for lucky number 13.

Sure, in many cases, optimism is a good thing. Studies show that optimistic people tend to live longer. They have an easier time making friends and attracting romantic partners. They also tend to be more charismatic. But optimism isn't all sunshine and roses. The downside of optimism is that people tend to downplay the negatives even in the face of evidence.

As discussed, a secular bear market, defined as an extended period of volatility and zero net growth, often lasts twenty years or longer. So let me ask you: Do you think that during each of those secular bear cycles, 100 percent of investors eventually pulled 100 percent of their money out of growth strategies? Of course not. Many stayed invested. It wasn't the pessimists who knew bad times could get worse, but the optimists who always thought recovery was right around the corner.

Again, it's one thing if you're young and still in the accumulation phase of your career. If you're in or near the income phase, you can't afford to let your bias toward optimism influence the financial decisions that affect your livelihood.

INVESTING THROUGH THE REARVIEW MIRROR

Fortunately, due to heroic government and central bank efforts, the US stock market surpassed its previous high set in 2000 and began to skyrocket again in 2013. As highlighted in chapter 4, during the next five to six years, the stock market nearly doubled. And from its

2009 lows, it quadrupled. Then it happened again after the beginning of the pandemic.

Psychologists would say that this is where recency bias kicks in, the tendency to extrapolate the recent past out into the future. It means that if the market is falling, one thinks it will continue to fall. If it's rising, it will continue to rise. I call this "investing through the rearview mirror" because it skews our perception and takes our attention away from what really matters. Unfortunately, the rearview mirror isn't even the mirror that lets you see that far behind, but rather your side-view mirror, with the warning label "objects may be closer than they appear." Optimism plays a role in this, too. For many investors, when the markets are shrinking, optimism can overpower our recency bias, at least in the early stages of a bear market. When markets are climbing, optimism and recency bias team up to blind even the most rational investors.

GROWTH VERSUS RETURN

I realize it's hard to quit growth stocks when they're hot, or at any time really. When you're up, you want to ride the wave higher. When you're down, you hope stocks will turn around so you can make up for lost ground. It's the same sort of addiction that affects drug users, smokers, gamblers, you name it.

We need to remember an important point: Whether you're investing for growth or investing for income, at the end of the day, there's only one thing we're all looking for, and that's a return on our investment.

But for many investors, all they can ever think about is the "G," half of TR=I+G, and it shows. Several times a week, an investor, retired or approaching retirement, will tell me that they are looking for growth on their money.

What they fail to remember is that growth is just one of the avenues for seeking return. It doesn't have to be the be-all and end-all. To illustrate this, I usually pitch a hypothetical scenario to my clients. Say I could get you an FDIC-insured CD that guarantees it will pay you 10 percent a year. Would that sound OK?

Of course it would.

There's just one problem. If you're looking for growth, which is really just another term for capital appreciation, then a CD won't work. They don't "grow," they just pay interest. It's all income.

You can see how silly this scenario is. Of course, this is a purely hypothetical situation. No FDIC-insured[56] CD pays 10 percent interest. If it did, I'd stop writing this book and tell you to throw every last cent you have into it.

I want to make this point crystal clear because it's very important. When people say they want more "growth" on their money, what they really mean is that they want more return. At the end of the day, most investors don't care whether it comes from the growth or the income, although those in or near retirement should. When they learn that the "I" is a more consistent and secure way of getting return than the "G," they prefer it, especially when they're at or near retirement age and are quite literally battling with time.

It just requires a change of mindset. It requires tweaking your thinking from "growth" to "return." Education helps, but addiction to growth is still hard to break.

OVERCOMING ADDICTION

If you were from my mom's generation, you probably smoked, and all your friends probably smoked as well. You did it for two reasons. The second is that nicotine relaxes you. The first is that it made you look cool.

In some respects, I would have loved to have been an ad man for cigarette companies in the 1940s and 1950s. I'd be willing to bet it was the easiest job in the world. The stuff practically sold itself.

I probably wouldn't have liked it so much when, in the 1960s onward, research started to come out by the truckload detailing the harmful effects of nicotine on the body and smoke in the lungs. I'm sure I would have hated myself even more in the 1970s and 1980s when those same people I raised on cigarettes started dropping like flies, rivaling the AIDS[57] epidemic.

My mom was one of those people. She started smoking in the early 1950s. At first, she did it because it felt good. By the time all the research started coming out two decades later, it didn't matter. She was already hooked. She was addicted. She didn't smoke because it felt good. She did it because she had to.

Here's a couple facts: Between 1960 and 1990, deaths by lung cancer increased by 500 percent. In 1987, lung cancer surpassed breast cancer to become the leading cause of death among US women.[58]

Today, smoking cigarettes is so uncool that many college campuses won't let you do it, and those that do will typically confine you and your cigarette-smoking buddies to a small box on the far south side of the campus.

The way I see it, the cycle moves in three stages:

1. Fun

2. Withdrawal

3. Sobriety

Stage One: In the early days, people smoked because they felt and looked cool.

Stage Two: Decades later, those who still smoked did it because they had to; they were addicted. They didn't smoke to feel good. They smoked so they wouldn't feel bad.

Stage Three: Today, everyone knows cigarettes are bad and most people try to stay away from them.

It's taken a long time for our society and our culture to reach stage three. It's literally taken decades and at least two generations. Now that we're here, there's no going back. The tide has shifted. People have more sense now, and cigarettes will never hold the place in our society that they once did.

I don't know if someday we'll feel the exact same way about "growth-only" strategies. With cigarettes, we have a symbol, lung cancer, that is embedded in the hearts and minds of people. We can link it to physical death. Financial death is a bit more abstract, but it's all the more threatening.

We know what stage one was—the fun and thrill of the 1980s and 1990s bull market. Growth stocks were the new game in town, and suddenly, they were the only game in town. People who had once never invested a dime in stocks or stock mutual funds, within years, were quitting their day jobs to become full-time day traders. Then came stage two: withdrawal. The markets lost half their value, twice. Trillions of dollars in market capitalization gone, vanished, poof. Have we crossed into stage three? Have we woken up? Are we ready to get sober yet? I'd like to think so, but it doesn't seem like it.

Rather than going into withdrawal, growth stocks have been jacked up on financial leverage like artificially low interest rates, corporate buybacks, and rising debt levels. We're still riding the high of the 1980s and 1990s like a nicotine addict who, instead of kicking the habit, switched to Nicorette gum, or worse, a vape pen.

The only difference with our culture's addiction to growth at all costs is that it began much later, and that's why it hasn't yet come full circle. But I think another secular bear market might push us over the edge into stage three.

As with cigarettes, it wasn't until enough people started literally dying when the masses woke up, revolted, and demanded tighter regulations and more transparency on the risks of smoking cigarettes.

What do you think will happen to our society if retirees are taking withdrawals, the market takes another 50 percent dive, and takes fourteen years to recover once again?

Do you think we'll be just as angry as we were after 2008? Do you think we'll be angrier? How many times will our culture allow this to happen before the people finally say "enough"?

Over the next ten to twenty years, I suspect we're going to see a radical shift as our generation, the Income Generation, comes to terms with the fact that we've been addicted to a drug that could financially kill us if we don't break the habit.

Eventually, it will happen. The party always ends. The gravy train stops rolling. The bottom line is cigarette smokers had twenty to thirty years after the "cool" days of the 1940s and 1950s before large-scale reports surfaced about the medical risks of smoking. Now those reports are taken for granted. As more suffer a financial death from utilizing cancerous financial strategies, talk about investing for the "I" will soon become the norm. When that happens, Retirement Income Source will be there.

CHAPTER 7

WHY DOESN'T MY "ADVISOR" TALK LIKE THIS?

I'm a blunt person, I always have been, and frankly, it's one of my greatest assets. When people talk to me, they know right away I'm telling it like it is. I'm a very different kind of financial advisor, because most want you to risk your money to get a return. They'll talk about hypotheticals and dance around the risk so you either ignore it or brush it off. Me, I put the risk front and center. I'm not trying to fool anyone.

Some would say it's a bad sales tactic. After all, greed sells. On the contrary, I've built up one of the largest operations that focuses on income in the country simply because I'm willing to tell my clients the things their typical advisor never will.

First, let's differentiate between the two types of "advisors" you've likely been exposed to. First is your commission-based salesperson or broker, and the second is a fee-based advisor. The former is really just that, a salesperson, not really an advisor.

In fact, when a broker helps you invest, they are held to what is known as a "suitability" standard. In other words, they are disallowed from making any recommendations that are blatantly wrong for you and your goals; as long as the recommendation is considered "suitable," then the broker has done his job.

The latter, on the other hand, is considered legally to be an advisor and is held to a fiduciary standard. In other words, they must make for you what they believe is the absolute best recommendation for your goals, essentially acting as a fiduciary under the law. In the real world, many advisors are licensed to act in both capacities, and often the customer isn't fully aware of the capacity in which they are acting for each transaction.

COMMISSION-BASED BROKERS

Unfortunately, the suitability standard is quite broad. For example, taking income using the withdrawal method, even if in a fairly high percentage, is typically not considered a violation of the standard, never mind the fact that it means they're depleting your principal. Or consider this: In the eyes of the regulators, it is still considered "suitable" for a ninety-year-old with nearly 100 percent of his or her money in "growth-only" strategies, or for that same investor holding thirty-year bonds that won't mature until long after they're dead. It sounds crazy, but it's true. In fact, it's worse than that.

Every commission-based broker has to be licensed with a brokerage firm, whose job it is to enforce the suitability standard. According to the laws of agency,[59] because they are considered acting as an agent of the agency, a broker's primary obligation is to his brokerage firm with whom he has an agency contract, not his customer.

Think for a moment about what that means. Let's say there are two possible recommendations that a broker can make to the client, both of which are considered suitable. One is really good for the client and reasonably good for the firm. The other is really profitable for the firm, even though it is slightly less beneficial to the client. Guess which recommendation, according to the laws of the agent/agency, he or she should make?

You guessed it, the one that fulfills his agency's legal requirements. By their nature, brokers do not have the best interest of their customers in mind, but rather the brokerage firm they're operating under. Sure, there are some brokers that thumb their noses at their supervisors and truly do what they believe is the best thing for their clients. But if you are the customer, can you ever be 100 percent sure?

WALL STREET'S CANCER

It gets worse still. I use cancer as a metaphor because it is so fitting. Cancer begins in the human body as one mutated cell. As it spreads, it goes off in any and all directions until it affects the entire body. The same can be said about certain aspects of Wall Street.

Let's say that you are now the CEO of a major brokerage firm with millions of customers and tens of thousands of shareholders to whom you answer. Do you know to whom YOUR fiduciary responsibility would be? You can probably guess—to your shareholders, not your firm's customers.

In fact, that's true with any firm that has shareholders. For example, if you were the CEO of General Motors,[60] your job is to help your company sell more GM automobiles so that it can make as much profit for the shareholders as possible. This means that any marketing information that your research department distributes does not have to be unbiased. Of course, we expect it to be highly favorable toward GM. The dealership owners or sales managers are happy to follow suit and focus on the positives of GM automobiles, as are the salespeople. That is how they make money, by selling more GMs.

So, if it turns out after the fact that a GM vehicle was not ideal for you, then you really can't blame the CEO, the research and marketing department, the sales manager, or the salesperson. After all, they were just doing their jobs. The blame is really yours because you went into the wrong dealership.

Now let's be clear: I have a GM car. It's actually my favorite vehicle. But even if it weren't, at the end of the day, it wouldn't be that big of a deal if it was the wrong car for me. I would just live with it until my next vehicle.

The trouble is, this same business model extends to Wall Street where we're not talking about a $20,000–$30,000 vehicle, but your entire life savings.

Now to be fair, in the brokerage industry, the regulators do really try to correct this by saying that any marketing needs to be "fair and balanced." In other words, it needs to be as close to unbiased as possible. And yes, if you were to read the ENTIRE prospectus (often more than one hundred pages), you would get the full story.

But when was the last time that you actually did that?

If you answered "never," then unfortunately you are among the vast majority of investors. Over the years as I have tried to get clients to read the prospectus, they would say, "If I have to read that entire book, and could understand it, then I wouldn't need you." In the real world, much of the broker-customer communication is verbal and unmonitored, and most of what your broker will tell you is whatever sales pitch he picked up from his or her research department.

SO WHAT'S STOPPING THEM FROM GIVING ME WHAT I NEED?

You might be wondering why brokerage firms would not want to promote income-based investing. After all, if there's a market for it, they can probably sell it, right?

They can. But there's often more money in growth strategies and stocks. And remember, the company's management has a fiduciary responsibility to its shareholders, not to its customers. If it's more profitable to sell one thing over another, that's what they're going to do. Consider this: If a brokerage firm sells you a mutual fund or a variable annuity, there is typically 5 percent or so distributed to the firm, the manager, the broker. That's $5,000 on a $100,000 sale.

That's not a bad shake. But they can do even better.

If, instead, they sell you on the concept of individual stocks, the commission would be less per transaction. However, that portfolio of individual stocks needs to be watched a bit more closely and more actively managed.

That means they won't just charge a commission on the one-time sale, but any time they need to buy and sell out of the individual stock, potentially triggering an even bigger revenue stream for the firm than the mutual fund or variable annuity sale over time. Also, the commission on individual securities is flexible and can be negotiated, whereas on the mutual fund or variable annuity it's usually fixed.

The point being, whether it's a mutual fund, variable annuity, or a portfolio of individual stocks, the brokerage firm can make good money. The rewards are potentially higher on a portfolio of stocks, but even on the other securities, they can still make 5 percent.

Now let's look at how that compares to a portfolio of individual bonds.

For brokers, bonds are normally considered a one-and-done type of investment. If you buy a ten-year bond, a broker can only charge you once during the life of that bond, meaning over a ten-year period, he gets paid only once.

Not only that, but since a bond is not considered speculative, he might feel as though he cannot charge as high a commission as a stock. The more speculative the investment, the higher the potential reward, and the higher the potential reward, the higher a broker can often justify in fees. With bonds, we're not going for broke. We're investing for the income. Barring a default, it's a steady Eddie contract designed to get us the exact income we need for our purpose-based goals and nothing more. That's why lower commissions are more or less baked into the cake. Consider this example. Let's say you go to your typical broker and you want to buy $100,000 worth of bonds. You might think $100,000 is a lot of money. On the sales side, the commission side, it's typically going to translate to about 0.5 percent, just $500.

That's it. One $500 payment for an investment that's going to sit there and do nothing for five or ten years or longer.

As you can imagine, your typical broker can't make a living doing that. He can make a living buying and selling stocks. After all, stocks have to be more actively managed. Every time he buys or sells a stock, he might be able to collect a full 1 percent.

What sounds better? Collecting 0.5 percent once every ten years? Or 5 percent by selling a mutual fund or variable annuity? Or 1 percent once, twice, maybe even three or four times a year by buying and selling stocks?

That's one of the reasons there aren't as many people in this business who specialize in buying bonds and bond-like investments for their clients. There's a much less sinister side to it as well. Let's face it. The stock market can be much more fun and exciting than bonds. This means that, for many, they provide the path of least resistance in financial sales.

What sounds more attractive to you? With growth strategies, you have unlimited upside potential. Over the long run, growth stocks average a 10 percent return, but there have been many years where it has grown by 20 or 30 percent. Then there are high-dividend-value stocks which, because of the dividends, might have less growth potential, or bonds and bond-like investments, where the best you will ever do is earn an interest of maybe 5 or 6 percent. That's it. Most growth-based businesses already have a much easier time selling you on their model. Then there is our perennial sense of optimism that we have already discussed. Even though you know in your heart that, technically speaking, you can lose 100 percent of your investment, it's easy to ignore the downside and focus on the upside. It is the same temperament that historically has kept growth-based investors all in during volatile, zero-growth, and twenty-year secular bear-market cycles.

IT'S ALL IN THE NAME

There is a reason that stockbrokers are called stockbrokers, because they typically favor stocks. You show me a real estate broker that says real estate is a bad investment and I will show you a stockbroker who says the same about stocks. It's typically the more aggressively minded individuals that gravitate toward becoming stockbrokers in the first place.

Think about it. If I were your school guidance counselor and you came to me describing yourself as a really, really conservative individual, do you think that I would ever recommend that you start a career as a stockbroker?

Probably not. So why then do many brokers describe themselves as being "conservative"?

Because, in essence, the word "conservative" is just a word. It means different things to different people. I'm sure that you know some extremely conservative people who would never dream of becoming a private pilot because they are just plain too conservative. But, if you were to ask a commercial airline pilot if he is aggressive or conservative, how do you think he'd respond? Conservative. Because he has hundreds of people on board, and because compared to his friend who is an aerobatic stunt pilot and nephew who is a military fighter pilot, he is conservative. It's just a word. It means different things to different people.

A commercial airline pilot is still a pilot of a 200-ton airplane. Nothing about flying an aluminum juggernaut at 30,000 feet is particularly conservative. Put the average person in the cockpit and they'd short-circuit from the pressure and responsibility. So it's very telling, for example, that even commercial pilots become immune to turbulence because they experience it much more often than the rest of us. I believe that, in a similar way, many stockbrokers become immune to risk since virtually every day the market is open, they have some customer who is losing money in some investment. They can become immune to risk and define "conservative" differently from most.

It goes to show you that when stockbrokers call stocks a safe or "conservative" investment, you should take it with a grain of salt.

HOW CANCER SPREADS HORIZONTALLY

So far I've talked about how Wall Street's cancer spreads vertically, from the CEO to the research department to the marketing department to the sales manager and finally to the salesperson, your broker. But cancer in the human body tends to spread in all directions. So how does Wall Street's cancer spread horizontally? The answer lies within the following question: "Does the media, including television, radio, and print, make most of their money from subscriptions or advertising?"

If you said "advertising," you would be correct.

Again, money talks. Just as a CEO or board of directors is beholden to their shareholders, media organizations are beholden to the advertisers that keep them in business. As you might expect, brokerage firms as well as other financial companies are the primary advertisers in the various forms of financial media.

Imagine that you were the chief marketing officer of a brokerage firm and had to choose which marketing media firm you would prefer to spend your firm's dollars—one that typically leads investors toward lower profit income strategies, or the higher profit margin approaches that your firm espouses? The answer is clear. Although the media in theory is unbiased (which we know it's not), media firms still need to stay in business and often have shareholders to which they answer. Their messages are often indirectly affected by their advertisers. They need those advertising dollars from your broker's firm.

Some believe that the "cancer" spreads even further horizontally to the schools that train financial advisors. To stay in business, these schools rely on brokerage firms and the like to encourage their representatives to attend. Would they still do that if what was being taught was contrary to their companies' interests? Moreover, many of these schools were initially funded and continue to be funded by those very same firms.

I saw the implications firsthand of how this can create bias.

As you saw in my bio, I have an alphabet soup after my name: David J. Scranton, CFA®, CFP®, ChFC, CLU.

When I was studying for one of these credentials more than two decades ago, I was learning a new "science" of investing, an extension of the Modern Portfolio Theory,[61] which allowed an advisor to mathematically mitigate much of a client's portfolio risk through certain types of diversification, almost like financial alchemy of sorts. I was skeptical because it didn't account for human emotions in investing even though it looked great on paper, until over the last two decades, when it failed to protect investors not once, but twice, in the real world.

Do you want to know what many of these schools are still teaching students today? Yup, you guessed it—the same thing.

The point being, the cancer doesn't just spread vertically through brokerage firms. It spreads horizontally to the media and the schools that educate financial advisors.

FEE-BASED FINANCIAL ADVISORS

Surely, Wall Street's cancer can't spread everywhere, you might think. After all, registered investment advisors are at least in theory supposed to act in the best interest of their clients, whereas stockbrokers have a fiduciary duty to their firm. Legally speaking, these advisors act as fiduciaries for their clients.

That puts a lot of people at ease. Many investors feel a greater sense of comfort knowing that they pay a fee instead of a commission for investment advisory services.

The theory is that the advisor earns more money if the client's account grows and less if it shrinks. Also, the advisor earns the same amount of money whether he makes more trades or fewer trades. It doesn't matter if he holds a particular investment for ten years or changes it several times per year. The fee is the same, whereas with brokers, there's a potential conflict of interest because they make more money the more they trade, regardless of the outcome. Alternatively, many investors take solace because, at least in theory, they and their advisor's goals are aligned. They're "sitting on the same side of the table," so to speak. While all this is true, most still don't espouse the principles in this book.

I cannot answer the "why" for every investment advisor in America because I don't know every single one of them. I'm also not a mind reader. And this is where Wall Street's cancer can afflict not just brokers but investment advisors alike.

CANCER SPREADS EVERYWHERE

Like brokers, financial advisors realize that the riskier the portfolio, the more active management is required. Many feel that more active management helps them justify a higher fee. Most advisors charge fees in excess of 1 percent of the assets being managed.

So let's say that your advisor had you invested in an extremely conservative portfolio of nicely laddered government bonds, so there was no default risk and no active management required. Tell me, how long would you want to pay a 1 percent fee to that advisor before you said, "Enough?" For sure, this is an extreme example, but do you get my point? The fee may not be so bad when double-digit returns are possible and at stake, but if your interest payment is only 3 percent, and the advisor takes 1 of that 3 percent, you're only netting 2 percent. Your advisor is earning one-half as much as you. Of course, most advisors don't have their clients heavily invested in income-first strategies because they themselves aren't familiar with them. They put them in growth-first strategies because that's the business they know. Many of these guys were stockbrokers before they became advisors.

True to the point, most fee-based accounts managed by investment advisors that I stumble across seem to have at least 50–70 percent invested in growth stocks or mutual funds, even for retirees or those nearing retirement. I am always amazed, wondering just how this one-size-fits-all solution can be considered to have fulfilled one's fiduciary duty. Hopefully, if you got this far in this book, you're wondering the same.

Basic Modern Portfolio Theory, the "alchemy" I described before, is considered by many to still be the "gold standard" today. It attempts to evaluate return versus volatility risk for all the different stocks and bonds or combinations. Combined with "Monte Carlo" math (discussed in chapter 3), it creates something called the "efficient frontier,"[62] which takes all the various stock/bond combinations to find the one that, in theory, results in the most return for the risk taken. According to that model, the "efficient frontier" only includes portfolios that have 40 percent or more in stocks or stock funds. Meaning no portfolios with less than 40 percent in stocks or stock funds are considered "efficient," regardless of income needs.

This may work in a theoretical world, where people have an indefinite period for which they can hold their investments or won't need much income in the future. In the real world, when they retire and need more income, it often doesn't. Some investors who want more income might need to reduce their stock exposure well below 40 percent to generate it, especially if they hold "growth-only" stocks. The problem is that the Modern Portfolio Theory bases all its returns on total return, with absolutely no differentiation between income and growth. In other words, it assumes that people get their cash flow utilizing the withdrawal method, not the income method.

So as an advisor, you might think that with more than 50 percent in growth strategies:

- Clients might be willing to pay you higher management fees.
- You have less regulatory and legal risk adhering to the "Gold Standard" of the investment markets.
- You have a sexier, more exciting business model.
- You can use mutual funds or ETFs and simplify your business.

It's a home run for you. It could be a strikeout for some of your clients.

LAZINESS, PURE AND SIMPLE

Let's admit it together: Human beings tend to be inherently lazy. We're the smartest creatures in the animal kingdom, and as such, we know how to work smarter, not harder, so we can relax more. We tend to take the path of least resistance whenever possible. Since advisors are human beings, it should be no surprise that this tendency affects them also.

This may seem hard to believe, but today most investment advisors don't really manage money at all. Some, vis-à-vis my fourth bullet point above, utilize mutual funds or ETFs. These funds have fund managers who actually do the money management within each fund so your advisor doesn't have to. All your advisor has to do is choose the right combination of funds and rebalance them occasionally, leaving a lot of leftover time to focus on growing his or her business.

Here's the problem with that. In the case of mutual funds especially, there tends to be higher fees, and I don't mean the fee you are paying your advisor; I am referring to the embedded fees inside the mutual fund. The fees that you forget about because they are not readily visible unless you look on page 87 of the prospectus.

Imagine if your auto mechanic couldn't fix your car, so he charged you a referral fee to send you to the proper mechanic whom you would then have to pay a separate fee to repair your vehicle. That's two sets of fees for one job. My friend Greg Melia (the chicken and egg guy) says advisors have essentially gotten so lazy that all they want to do is check off a box on an application, which is all it really takes for one to invest your dollars in a mutual fund. Then they try to convince you that doing nothing is OK. He calls it "The Disease of Ease."[63]

Granted, there are some advisors who include individual stocks in client portfolios, but many of them still don't really do any money management. Often, they have anywhere from five to ten different preset portfolios that they utilize. For example, they might have one that has 100 percent stock, another that has 80 percent stocks and 20 percent bonds, one that is 60/40 or 40/60, and so on. They normally ask you to complete a "risk tolerance questionnaire." Then they input your answers into a computer algorithm, which then determines the portfolio that best fits you. Done. Simple, painless; your money gets invested in the pool and your advisor is off to search for his next client. The only problem is that the portfolio was probably chosen based on the Modern Portfolio Theory and other factors, none of which differentiates between the "Income" and the "Growth." Again, "The Disease of Ease." Does that sound like adherence to a fiduciary standard to you?

GROWTH STOCK CHEERLEADERS

Cheerleaders have one job, to cheer. It doesn't matter if their team is winning or losing. They cheer regardless because that is what cheerleaders do.

The same is true for most brokers and advisors. They're growth stock cheerleaders. When are you more excited to invest in the stock market[64] for growth? Is it when markets are climbing and everyone is optimistic or when markets are declining and pessimism abounds? The answer is obvious. Optimism is contagious! The cheerleaders know this. In many ways, they are in the business of selling optimism.

This might explain why, when markets are climbing, you are told that it is a good time to invest, but when markets are down you are told that it is a great chance to buy low. No matter the situation, they want you to think it's always a great time to buy.

Now be honest with yourself. When you read chapter 4 about these long-term secular market cycles, wasn't it the first time that you've heard these cycles discussed so succinctly? How predictable and repeatable do they seem to have been throughout history?

Whenever I present that historical data, I typically hear, "So shouldn't we just get out of the market for those twenty years or so of bear-market cycles?" Brokers and advisors know that wouldn't be good for their business.

THE INFORMATION'S GOT TO COME FROM SOMEWHERE

Even totally "independent" brokers and advisors fall into this trap.

Let's say, for example, that a broker is registered with a smaller independent family-owned brokerage firm (not one of the big brokerage houses that have to answer to shareholders). That smaller firm probably cannot afford to have its own research department. That broker is then expected to do his own research.

The only problem is that he is unlikely to have enough time available to do that. Between prospecting for new clients, servicing existing clients, maybe doing paperwork, keeping up with compliance requirements, actually meeting with prospects or clients, and managing his office, research often falls to the bottom of the list. Even if that broker has two or three full-time employees, that is a lot to ask.

So most get their research by purchasing it from an outside source. Some are "lucky" enough that their firms actually pay for it. But where do you think that research typically comes from in the first place?

Bingo.

The original source of most of this information is tied directly or indirectly to the larger brokerage firms, those who do have to answer to shareholders. This is referred to as "sell-side" research.

What about independent investment advisors? After all, they are fiduciaries. True, except that they have the same time limitations as those with an independent brokerage house, maybe worse. Most attempt to do some research on their own but ultimately need the help of an outside source, similar to those that are available to brokers.

In other words, they both fall into the same trap.

Remember, brokers and advisors are human beings, susceptible to all the same emotional factors affecting those of you who manage your own investments. Optimism, check. Recency bias, check.[65] A stock market paradigm if he or she got into the industry between 1980 and 2000, 2003 and 2007, or after 2009, check. Finally, susceptible to addictions where the longer the addiction, the more difficult the recovery, check.

Unless they struggle with an affliction such as Asperger's, humans make decisions emotionally first, and only then do we attempt to justify them logically. It is simply how 99 percent of all humans are wired, regardless of professional training.

DON'T GET SWEPT UP BY THE HERD

Like sheep, many "advisors" today think there is no other way. They invest for growth because it's the only thing they've been taught, and, ultimately, they follow the herd over a cliff.

That may not be fair to sheep. Sheep get a bad reputation for being the stupidest animals on earth. The reality is that sheep are surprisingly intelligent. They have long memories, they remember faces, and they form bonds with their friends and masters. They also feel sadness when one of their own gets sent to the slaughter.

But herd mentality is very real. It's been studied in both humans and animals. We're all programmed, on some level, to do what everyone around us is doing, even if it flies in the face of common sense and puts us in grave danger.

For decades, the herd rode the growth wave to great riches. It was all advisors knew. Then when the party ended, they stayed in because it was still all they knew.

Essentially, they have forgotten that return, your total return, is made up of two components, growth and income.

> **AS I EXPLAINED EARLIER, WRITTEN OUT, THE FORMULA LOOKS LIKE THIS:**
> **TR = I + G**

Once again, write that down. Put it on a small piece of paper. Stick it in your wallet and commit it to memory. Total return equals income plus growth.

It may sound like a simple formula, but the majority of investors, brokers, and advisors alike have forgotten this simple equation after years and years of programming to feel differently. We've been taught that the only way to make return is through the "G," through growth.

But the entire point of this book is to teach you why that simply isn't true, and to further teach you how switching your investment focus from the "G" to the "I"—to income—can help you achieve your retirement goals with greater certainty and much less stress.

CHAPTER 8

HAVE YOU OUTGROWN YOUR CURRENT ADVISOR?

I loved my doctor growing up. Most children hate going to the doctor. For most parents it's like herding cats, or, God forbid, trying to give one a pill.

Not me. I loved my pediatricians. In fact, everyone loved them. Dr. Becker and Dr. Glass were the best of the best. I loved them so much that by the time I was twenty, I was still going to them.

It must have been quite a sight. There I was, a twenty-year-old bodybuilder, six feet tall, 270 pounds, surrounded by a bunch of children and still going to see my pediatrician. I didn't mind it so much. My doctors were great. As the old saying goes: if it ain't broke, don't fix it.

The fact is, I had outgrown them, and I didn't want to accept it. So eventually, the doctors called me up one day and broke the news. They told me I had to select a primary care doctor. An adult primary care doctor.

I didn't like it at first. No one likes change when it's forced on them. But in time, I came to like my new doctor just fine.

Now, I share this rather silly and frankly embarrassing story with you to illustrate a point. When it comes to our finances, there are people who specialize in the growth or the accumulation phase of our wealth, just as there are pediatricians who specialize in treating growing children. It's a mistake to assume that the same financial doctor who helped you grow your investments is the same one who can help you generate income during your income years. It's as silly as going to a pediatrician until you're twenty years old.

My doctor today, Dr. Gaudio, is just as good as the doctors I had when I was little. I love going to see him. But one of these days, I'm going to outgrow him, too. Eventually my health will start to decline, and I'll have to seek out a doctor who specializes in geriatric medicine. I won't like it. I probably won't make the choice of my own volition. One of these days, Dr. Gaudio is going to call me into his office and tell it to me straight. *Dave, it's time to get a new doctor.*

It's the same with money; except you'll never find an advisor who will tell you to go somewhere else (unless you put your foot down that you're only interested in generating interest and dividends in the 4–5 percent range or greater). There are financial advisors who specialize in growth and there are advisors who specialize in income, just as there are doctors who treat adults and those who treat the elderly. What is right for one is not necessarily right for the other. The fact is, unless you're in Florida, there are a LOT more doctors who treat regular-aged adults than there are those who treat senior citizens, and of those doctors, there are only a few good ones.

They are out there and finding the right one can literally mean the difference between life and death.

It's the same with finding a true income-first advisor. There are a lot of growth advisors out there. There are even fewer income advisors, and of the ones available, there are only some who know how to manage a portfolio of income-generating strategies the Dave Scranton way.

I say this as a person who has spent much of my career specializing in this smaller niche of the market, as well as building up a national network of advisors who do the same.

It's as simple as this—the advisor you may have worked with for the past twenty years helping you grow your assets is not the advisor you want to help you protect your assets, and he's probably not the best one to help you generate your "I."

BONDS AND BOND-LIKE INSTRUMENTS, THE RIGHT WAY

If you take nothing else from this book, I want you to really highlight this next section. I'm serious. Get a Post-it note. Earmark the page. Do something so you don't forget this.

As discussed in chapter 7, it's true that a broker can't make a living buying $100,000 worth of individual bonds and bond-like investments for his clients. It's too much work for most because they can only charge a very small fee, and only do it once for the life of the bond. But $100,000 is still a lot of money. Your advisor still wants to have it under his management. So, rather than buy a basket of individual bonds, he's going to put you in something called a "bond mutual fund."

Sounds OK, right? Everyone loves mutual funds,[66] and we know bonds are more conservative investments.

Most investors will be OK with this. In fact, this is what most likely happens the majority of the time when an investor approaches a financial advisor and says they want to put their money in bonds.

There's just one problem: It's not a bond. It's a bond mutual fund.

So when your typical investor hears the term "bond mutual fund," it checks off two boxes in his head.

1. He knows he needs bonds.
2. He knows he likes mutual funds.

Here's what he doesn't know: A bond mutual fund gives you neither of the two guarantees that make a diversified portfolio of individual bonds attractive (assuming no defaults) but contains all the risks of mutual funds. In fact, if you were to study for the examination to become an investment advisor, the textbook would say that a bond fund is really not a bond at all; it is the stock of a company that owns bonds. It sounds even riskier.

This is one of my biggest challenges as a financial advisor. As a population, we have mutual fund addiction. When I ask people which instrument they think would be safer, a bond or a bond mutual fund, they're going to tell me the latter because that's what they were taught. But it's wrong.

FIXED PAYMENTS

Here's the difference between buying a stock and buying a bond: When you invest for growth the only way you make money is when the investment goes up in value. At the end of the day, it's speculation. You're betting on the company and the management team in place. So back to our friend, the "bond mutual fund."[67] Remember those two guarantees we mentioned earlier in the book: barring default, a guaranteed amount of interest for the life of the bond and guaranteed repayment of principal at maturity? Great. Now forget them. Pretend they never existed. That, in short, is your bond fund.

A bond fund is simply a regular old mutual fund, except instead of investing in stocks, it pools its money in bonds. Many investment advisors consider it a simpler way of investing in bonds. You want to avoid those investment advisors, because they don't know what they're talking about.

FIXED INCOME INVESTING

MUTUAL FUNDS		INDIVIDUAL BONDS	
Fixed Income Rate	No	Fixed Income Rate	Yes
Definite Maturity	No	Definite Maturity	Yes
Return of Principal	No	Return of Principal	Yes
Management Fees	Yes	Management Fees	No
Know What You Own	No	Know What You Own	Yes

That's because, unlike bonds, when you buy into a bond mutual fund, there's no contract. With a bond, you know what you get, what you get back, and when you get it. If it's a two-year bond, you get your money back in two years. If it's a thirty-year bond, you get it back in thirty.

The payments are fixed. With a bond mutual fund, everything is variable.

THE DISEASE OF EASE

The solution, of course, is just to buy a portfolio of actual bonds—except, it's not that easy. As I explained, there's less money in it for a broker and possibly the advisor. Since money talks, and there's not a lot of money in bonds as far as advisors are concerned, there is a limited pool of experienced advisors who specialize in this field to choose from, at least compared to the wide pool of advisors who specialize in stocks. That means fewer of those with experience or with an already established clientele will be willing to take you on as a client. Worse, the ones who will take you on as a client might not know what they're doing, either.

Consider it like this: Have you ever met someone who is both an orthopedic surgeon and a chiropractor? Probably not. They're usually either one or the other. That's because each field requires a high degree of specialization, education, and experience. Anyone who's smart knows they shouldn't go to an orthopedic surgeon when what they really need is a chiropractor, and vice versa. It's the same in the financial industry. Advisors typically specialize in either the stock market or the bond market. Very few specialize in both, and the ones who do probably aren't renowned specialists in either.

I, for one, would be a terrible advisor to a thirty-year-old client with a $200,000 portfolio. That client doesn't want 5 and 6 percent investing for the "I." He wants 8–10 percent investing for the "G." Quite frankly, if he wants that, he needs to invest in growth stocks. I haven't focused on growth-based strategies in twenty-five years. My specialization since 1999 has been income, so I'm not his guy. We have others in the firm who can do that.

If you're fifty years old or older—in other words, at or near retirement age—I'm your guy, and if I'm not your guy for geographical reasons, I can put you in touch with someone who is your guy, because there aren't that many of us out there, at least compared to your typical investment advisor.

You have to remember that, for most investment advisors, their specialization—that is, the stuff they actually know—is growth, not income, meaning probably not bonds.

HAVE YOU OUTGROWN YOUR CURRENT ADVISOR?

So let me ask you this: If you need a knee replacement, and you know a chiropractor who is also an orthopedic surgeon and has successfully performed ten knee replacements to date, will you let him operate on you?

Maybe, if the price is right and he has another expert in the room who knows what he's doing. You also might have a really good lawyer who can make that kind of fiasco waiting to happen worth your while.

Otherwise, you likely wouldn't let him perform his eleventh surgery on you. While he may know how to perform the surgery, he's never going to be as good as the full-time orthopedic surgeon who has performed over 1,000 of these surgeries successfully with minimal marks on his otherwise seamless record. Chances are, if that chiropractor was good enough at his chiropractic work, he wouldn't have needed to double up. Both are very specialized fields that require years of training and experience.

So, too, for financial advisors, you can't expect an advisor who has spent his entire life dealing with growth to know what he's doing when he tries to apply his same skills to the bond market. Even he understands this, though he likely won't admit as much.

The problem is that investing in bonds the right way requires a great deal of skill, experience, and know-how.

Do you think those advisors learned any of that skill and know-how, as it pertains to the bond market, during the 1980s and 1990s when stocks were the only game in town? Not hardly, and that's why they buy bond mutual funds instead of a diversified portfolio of individual bonds. They wouldn't even know where to start.

You might think it's as easy as going to the US Treasury and buying a ten-year bond that pays a fixed rate of interest. Except Treasuries aren't what they used to be. Back in the early 1990s, you could still get 8 percent on a Ten-Year Treasury.

Today it's different. But that's OK, there are plenty of investments out there that will pay you more without risking your money on growth stocks.

However, if your advisor has been playing with growth stocks and mutual funds his whole life, it's probably safe to say he has no idea where to find them or how to negotiate a good price, let alone how to do good by his clients, including you.

That's why your typical advisor will put you in bond mutual funds when you say you want to shed some of the risk from your portfolio. He doesn't know how to do anything else.

Here again, it's the "Disease of Ease" and it's a disease that's spread throughout the entire financial industry. It looks pretty plain and simple on the one hand. They can't get the job done right. But on the other hand, the Securities and Exchange Commission (SEC)[68] won't come knocking on their door for putting their clients in bond funds, either.

Now you might wonder if good fixed-income investments are out there, and your advisor who is a fiduciary has to act in your best interest, how can they possibly get credit for merely putting their clients in bond funds that have none of the benefits of actual bonds?

It's a good question. The answer is simply because their clients don't know the difference (and because the advisors themselves may not know the difference). From a regulator's standpoint, interest rates in general had been declining from 1981 to 2014, providing bond mutual funds with a tailwind for a very long time. When things are going up, clients are happy even if they don't completely understand why.

All that changed around 2015 when interest rates started to climb due to the Fed's reversal of quantitative easing and other factors. The tailwind turned into a headwind and clients began to notice the effect on bond funds. Fortunately, you can use this knowledge to arm yourself.

WHAT SEPARATES US FROM EVERYONE ELSE

As mentioned earlier, most advisors know growth and that's it. Of the ones who will put your money in bonds, most will use bond funds, which really aren't bonds but more like the stock of a company that owns them. It gets you none of the benefits or potential guarantees that come with owning individual bonds while subjecting you to most of the same risks of owning stocks. So, what should you look for when you're searching for a good bond advisor?

There are five things a good bond advisor must do in order to manage a portfolio effectively. By effectively, I mean they must know how to help protect your wealth through a diversified portfolio of individually managed bonds and bond-like instruments that can generate over 5 percent in income every year so you never have to withdraw from your principal if you don't want to. Every advisor we have listed on the Retirement Income Source website must meet the following five criteria.

NUMBER 1

As you can probably guess by now, we don't use bond funds. We invest in individual bonds and bond-like investments. If an advisor can't get this first step right, then he or she doesn't really specialize in the "I." Period. This one criterion alone separates us from more than 90 percent of the advisory community out there. But we don't stop there, not even close.

NUMBER 2

Second, we look beyond the ratings agencies and examine the actual financials of the companies we are considering.

As shocking as it may seem, many advisors don't do this.

It's baffling considering the hard lesson learned in 2007 and 2008 that you cannot trust the ratings agencies to be honest with their creditworthy assessments. After all, they had issued countless AAA ratings on the very mortgage bonds that brought down the economy. If one rating agency wouldn't give the rating desired to the company in question, the bond issuer would simply go down the street to the other and get it. Because these agencies are "for-profit" businesses, they straddle a very fine line.

The result? You tend to FEEL safe because the ratings agencies issued a AAA rating, even if you are not. If you've ever seen the movie *The Big Short*, you know how this played out. There's this prescient moment in the movie when the protagonists talk it out with a female ratings agent. They ask, "Why would you give these bonds such a high rating if you knew the underlying assets were junk?" Her response: "If we didn't, the guys next door would."

Again, money talks. That's why we don't just look at a bond's rating. Sure, a AAA rating is great, but it's not enough. That's why we have to dig into the security's actual financial ratios for us to feel secure with the investment. It's like the old parable: You can have the sturdiest, most immaculate home in the world, but if it's resting on a bed of sand, it's no good. It has to be built on a firm foundation.

NUMBER 3

This is a big one. Third, we use limit orders.

Most financial advisors who do the first two steps will miss this one. They simply buy investments at whatever price the market is offering that day. They are in too much of a hurry to invest your money so they often overpay for it.

Limit orders are important for this very reason. You never want to overpay for your investments. By placing a limit order at a desired price level, we are simply waiting for an investment to drop to that level. When it does, the buy order triggers automatically without the potential for human error.

This can take days, sometimes weeks, but that's OK. You want to get the right price. It's one thing to do that with stocks, which can offer growth. By saving 1 or 2 percent, you make up that 1 or 2 percent when you eventually sell your stock. But it only happens once.

The difference with fixed-income investments is that you have to remember the interest or dividend is fixed. It means that by paying less, you can buy more; therefore, you will earn more interest each and every year that you hold the security. And not just once, like stocks, but every year. So, limit orders are important with growth stocks, but they are essential with income securities. You have to be very strategic when you're tackling the fixed-income market.

NUMBER 4

Fourth, we use Bloomberg technology. It's not cheap, but again, we're trying to get the best deal for our clients, which is why a good advisor must spend the time and resources to search for the best buying opportunities. We want to get the highest quality bonds with the highest potential yield.

The beauty of Bloomberg Terminals,[69] named after, of course, Michael Bloomberg himself, is that they give a bond manager a lot of transparency in the bond market specifically. This is helpful because the bond market, although bigger than the stock market, is less liquid than the stock market.

If you want to buy Apple stock, for example, you can be reasonably assured that you can get it for about the same price it was trading for five seconds ago, because it has a pretty large trading volume. The seller gets the money from the buyer and the commission is visible to both parties. Most large-cap stocks[70] are like this. They're that liquid and that transparent. That's because there are plenty of shares available at all times.

The bond market is different. For a given bond issue, there might be only a handful or less of real potential sellers at any particular moment, not millions of shares as is often the case with stocks. Sometimes, there are no particular sellers at all in a given day or possibly several days for that matter.

That's why I have several analysts that sit in front of a Bloomberg Terminal every hour the market is open so they can pounce on these opportunities. That brings us to the second part of this step.

We don't just have analysts sitting in front of a computer watching the market go by. When a bond issue goes up for sale, we often go directly to the seller to negotiate a fair price for our clients. You see, when a bond issue is for sale, they might "advertise" an asking price. Potential buyers can then bid on the bond similar to an auction. Traditionally, this is done through a clearinghouse, which is a company that has a seat on an exchange. There's a bid, there's an ask, and then there's negotiating until the seller finds the price he wants.

The clearinghouse in the middle is facilitating a settlement price on behalf of both parties. In exchange for this service, it is "marking up" the price of the bond.

When the transaction is complete, most sellers don't know what the buyer paid and most buyers don't know what the seller received.

One seller might be willing to sell the same bond for a lower price than the buyer is willing to pay. In this case, the middleman gets a windfall. In the stock market, on the other hand, shares are traded through an exchange so that every share of a particular stock or security trading at the same time trades for pretty close to the same price so the buyer and the seller get to keep the windfall for themselves. Also, the commission is often much smaller and completely transparent to both parties, that's the difference. Bloomberg technology tells us who is looking to sell a certain type of bond that we want to buy for our clients. It tells us the asking price without any middleman's markup. That's what is key. With that information in hand, we can go directly to the seller and negotiate a fair price. We can negotiate with different sellers at the same time to see who will give us the best price.

The reality is that, with this technology, we make bond purchases through our clearinghouse less than 10 percent of the time. And 90 percent of our bond trades happen as a direct result of using the technology to identify sellers and negotiate a fair price with them directly and a better price than we can typically get through the middleman.

Guess what happens when we wish to sell a particular holding. The same thing happens all over again, this time in reverse. The technology gives us the transparency we need to negotiate the highest price we can.

Most advisors won't do this. In fact, most can't. They don't have the resources or the personnel. Instead, they'll go straight to their clearinghouse and pay whatever price is on offer, including the middleman's markup. That's why it's important to have an advisor with the right infrastructure in place.

These may seem like small details, and some of them are, but for our clients, it can mean the difference of thousands of dollars per year in extra income. When it comes to bonds, every decimal point counts.

If we can get an extra 0.001 percent, we'll do it. Even if it's just a difference of a few hundred dollars, we go the extra mile, because it's our job. It's our mission to do right by our clients. And more importantly, it's just the right thing to do, period.

Number 5

Fifth and final, we actively manage our portfolios. This is what truly separates us from other advisors.

Between 1981 and 2014, interest rates were in a loosening cycle. That is, they were in an overall declining trend.

Generally speaking, as interest rates fall, bond prices tend to go up. This meant that, for more than thirty years, bonds and bond-like investments essentially had a tailwind. One could buy a bond and hold onto it knowing the price would more likely go up than down.

However, interest rates started rising after 2014. In an interest rate tightening cycle, one in which interest rates are rising, that tailwind turns into a headwind. It requires active management.

In this environment, the concept of buy low and sell high may be simple but it's not easy. It takes experience and know-how. Our advantage here is that we are one of the few willing to carry the fixed-income cross and, quite frankly, I'm one of the few people in the business who has been carrying it for the last twenty years. I know how this market works.

The stock market is said to be very "efficient," meaning that information today about any particular stock, including current pricing, is immediately available to anyone with a computer. This means that it is really difficult for anyone to have a trading advantage over another in the stock market. It's become more difficult for an investor to outperform the market than ever before. Liquidity and transparency lead to efficiency.

In the bond market, however, there's less liquidity. Less liquidity means less efficiency. This reduced efficiency creates what I refer to as dislocations in the bond market. These dislocations often provide for swap opportunities within our portfolios.

Let's say I own a block of a certain type of corporate bonds that pays a 5 percent yield. In theory, all similar bonds should go for the same price and offer the same yield, assuming the same ratings, same industry, same maturity, and so on.

But sometimes dislocations occur, meaning any one of these variables might be different for similar bonds. So, whereas every share of Apple trades for the same price, in the bond market, it's a little trickier.

For example, assume that some insurance company, for some reason, is trying to sell a big block of one of those bonds. To do so, it may have to "advertise" a slightly lower ask price. This means a slightly higher yield, perhaps 5.1 or 5.2 percent. That gives us an opportunity to sell the bonds we own that pay 5 percent, and buy the ones paying a slightly higher return at 5.1 or 5.2 percent. That's a difference that can add up and one of the many reasons I have my portfolio managers keep their eyes peeled for these opportunities.

The thing is, these dislocations may not happen often, but when they do, they may just last for a few hours, sometimes not even that. That's why we actively manage our portfolios to stay on top of any swap opportunities. That's why we have CFAs and other analysts who sit in front of a Bloomberg Terminal all day and do just that.

Most financial advisors can't afford to hire an analyst, let alone a CFA or team of CFAs, and they certainly don't have the time to sit in front of the terminal themselves. They have to see clients. So as a result, they miss the opportunity.

FOUR TYPES OF SWAPS

There are four types of swaps we look out for. I don't want to get too deep into the weeds here, but the first two swaps are designed to increase our return, and they are offensive measures. These are "pay me now" and "pay me later." The last two are more defensive. These are "cover my assets I" and "cover my assets II." And yes, I named them to be a bit tongue-in-cheek.

1. Pay me now. That's when we sell out of a block of bonds and bond-like instruments to buy different bonds and bond-like instruments with a better current yield. In other words, more interest today.

2. Pay me later. This is where we increase the yield to maturity. Unlike current yield, yield to maturity also accounts for any gain or loss between the purchase price and the face amount that will contractually be repaid at maturity. In other words, it represents the actual economic internal rate of return if held to maturity.

3. Cover my assets I. This swap decreases duration. In other words, it reduces our interest rate risk. Different bonds and bond-like instruments have different levels of susceptibility to changes in interest rates.

4. Cover my assets II. In this one, we reduce our credit risk. Credit risk refers to the chance that the issuer of the bond will default on its debt obligations. When we get the chance to help protect our clients, we take it.

That's it. Four types of swaps; pay me now, pay me later, cover my assets I, and cover my assets II; and our five rules for investing in bonds, which are:

1. Buy actual bonds and not bond funds.

2. Look beyond the ratings agencies.

3. Don't buy at the market; use limit orders instead.

4. Have a CFA utilize a Bloomberg Terminal to negotiate better prices instead of buying bonds through your clearinghouse.

5. Actually manage the portfolio as a financial advisor is supposed to do.

That's what makes our approach so effective and so different. It's possible that you'll never find a stock advisor who knows how to do this, and you'll be hard-pressed to find a bond advisor outside our network who can, either.

It isn't easy. It takes work. I compare it to climbing a rope in high school gym class. When you climb a rope, you get a few pulls in, then you wrap your feet around the rope so you don't slide back down. Then you rest. When you've caught your breath, you get a few more pulls in, then you wrap your feet and rest again. Pull, wrap, rest. That's what fixed-income investing is like. You get spurts of swap opportunities, and they slow down. The opportunities dry up. So you rest. Knowing that individual bonds are a contract with potential guaranteed terms is like wrapping your feet so you can't slide back down.

Or think of it like having a sailboat that only does six knots maximum speed, and that's if the wind cooperates. Sometimes it's a lot slower. So, let's say that one day you have no wind at all. If the current happens to be pushing you toward your destination no problem. But what if the current is moving against you? What do you do? Do you let it push you back? No. You drop anchor, wait for the current to pass. And we can do that because we're buying individual bonds; it is like dropping the anchor. Worst-case scenario, we hold our bonds to maturity and continue collecting the income on those investments. You drop anchor, you lock your legs, and you wait for the next opportunity. Let me be real with you. Even affluent investors have a hard time finding a fixed-income manager who is willing, or even knows how to do what we do. It's hard. It's really hard. It takes sacrifice. That's why I often refer to it as bearing the cross. There's not as much money in it for us, and frankly it's a lot more difficult. It's burdensome. It requires a mind toward doing what's right.

It would be a lot more profitable for me to take the easy road and use the old stock market model or, even better, just use bond funds. But remember, since the hyperinflation of the 1970s, interest rates had been falling. They'd been falling all the way through to the financial crisis when the Federal Reserve ultimately lowered overnight interest rates to zero percent and drove down long-term rates with quantitative easing. Bonds had a massive tailwind at their back, driving prices up. For more than thirty years, you could have just bought and held onto bonds knowing that interest rates were going down. When interest rates drop, bond prices tend to go up.

So when Fed Chair Janet Yellen announced in 2013 that the Fed was going to begin raising interest rates and reverse quantitative easing, it marked a shift for income-seeking investors. And it marked a shift in my business and my mission.

Now, we had to be more strategic. We had to actively manage these bonds and bond-like investments the way some advisors actively manage a portfolio of stocks. The only other option was to actively manage these portfolios as a broker, charging a half percent every time. I might actually make more money, except it wouldn't make sense for our clients. They would go broke with fees. That's why I switched toward the investment advisory model so I could actively manage these portfolios in a way that's cost-effective for my clients. The goal is to get them 5 percent a year. It's not so Mr. Advisor can get rich.

DIVIDEND STOCKS DONE THE RIGHT WAY

Many of the same risk management principles we use for investing in bonds and contract-based securities like REITs, BDCs, and annuities also apply when it comes to our approach to investing in common stocks. It's important to understand that, while common stocks do have a potential place in some retirees' portfolios, it's not the same place they would have in the portfolio of a younger person who has many years to ride out the market's peaks and valleys.

In previous chapters, we made it very clear we think the risks associated with growth-only investing are too high for people in and near retirement for two main reasons: (1) Because older investors may not have enough time left to recover from a potential major financial loss. (2) Because growth-only investments don't generate income, which is what retirees need most. As to the first point, it's worth noting that the average business cycle lasts six to seven years, so a person with a twenty- to thirty-year retirement is likely to see three to four market downturns and recoveries during that span. As to the second point, keep in mind that these downturns will be occurring at a time when that retirees' income from Social Security, pensions, and possible employment will likely be lower than his annual expenses. All of this is why preserving as much of your investment pool as possible to generate income is critical during retirement.

And not all downturns and recoveries are equal. In fact, the rolling average returns since 1900 have had periods of more than ten years before stock and bond investors got back to the break-even point in the worst-case scenarios. The impacts of these periods have been even worse for investors who did not collect interest and dividends along the way.

On the other hand, common stocks that do pay dividends have tended to be less volatile and have delivered higher returns over time than pure growth stocks or bonds—although not higher cash flows than bonds. And most importantly, they gave retirees much-needed income along the way. The chart below, courtesy of Ned Davis, illustrates the superior returns of dividend payers over nondividend payers from 1973 to 2022.

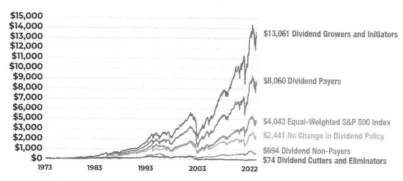

As with individual bonds, one of the reasons dividend-paying stocks have tended to outperform their all-growth peers is that their value is less sensitive to spikes in interest rates. This price durability occurs because when analysts are trying to determine the actual value of an investment, the dividend makes it possible to gauge that value more accurately, rather than having to predict it.

This is a fancy academic way of saying that dividends in the bank are worth more than promises down the road, and these "dividend deposits" can compound over time, just like interest earned on cash balances.

Another benefit of dividend-paying stocks as a class is that they are made up almost entirely of established businesses that can afford to pay dividends. This fact almost by default screens out more speculative businesses, or those whose valuation depends on sustaining above-average growth. More established, stable businesses tend to retain their value longer and their prices tend to be less volatile than emerging companies. Although emerging companies may offer the potential for higher rewards, they also carry higher risks.

WHY NOT JUST STICK WITH BONDS?

By now, some of you may be wondering if I've lost my mind or become schizophrenic. I can just hear you saying, "Dave, you just spent 100 pages railing against growth stocks but now you're saying OK to buying dividend-paying stocks, even though they carry more risk and yield less than the same company's bonds? Why bother? Why not just stick with bonds all the way?"

I ask myself the same question sometimes and the answer is twofold. First, stocks have historically delivered higher gross and after-tax returns than bonds. So, for investors with long retirements ahead of them, it might make sense to invest a portion of their portfolios in stocks—just so long as it's the lower risk, higher dividend variety. How much you may want to allocate to stocks depends on your individual needs, goals, and risk tolerance.

Secondly, stocks have a built-in inflation adjustment mechanism that bonds typically don't. The average rate of inflation over the last sixty years[71] has been 3.9 percent, and if that is the case in your retirement, it means every 18.5 years, your cost of living will double. So, to keep up with inflation, you either need your income to grow by 3.9 percent per year, or you need to decrease your spending by 3.9 percent. Most would prefer their income to grow, naturally. Stocks that pay dividends typically increase their dividends with their earnings. So, a company whose earnings are growing at 5 percent is likely to increase its dividend by the same amount, which, of course, is more than the average rate of inflation. So, what starts out as a lower payment than what the same company's bonds provide can often exceed that level before the end of your retirement, especially on an after-tax basis.

Also, those dividends can be reinvested to either increase your shares or purchase bonds along the way as a means of dollar cost averaging, which—of course—is another proven strategy to increase your rate of returns over time. Either way, the income from the stocks grows. Plus, it's taxed at a lower rate, for taxable accounts, than the interest paid on bonds.

STOCK ANALYSIS FOR GROWTH

Naturally, most professional stock investors (those that build portfolios by analyzing individual stocks) do a considerable amount of analysis before choosing which stocks to invest in. They start by looking at the financials: things such as the balance sheet, the income statement, and the cash flow statement. They make sure the company is healthy. They then do a 360-degree analysis and investigate a company's competitive offerings versus similar companies. They talk to customers, suppliers, competitors, and others, and seek to understand why a stock is trading where it is. They also seek to gauge what the consensus view of the company's future is, and why that view may or may not be correct. They also will consider technical indicators and other metrics on a stock's price to determine market sentiment about the stock, which can sometimes temporarily override financial fundamentals. They consider whether the company is in an industry that is growing or shrinking, and whether the company itself has a growing or shrinking share of its industry. The caliber and track record of the company's management and board are also important factors, especially how they allocate capital, incentivize managers, and view returning capital to shareholders.

STOCK ANALYSIS FOR DIVIDENDS

So, how does all this differ from how we invest for stocks with a focus on dividend income? In one sense there is no difference. We consider all these factors, too, but with a few extra twists. In addition to seeking companies with financial stability and the potential for improvement over time, we also look for reasons why a company should outperform the consensus view that Wall Street and investors have for its future. When we find enough reasons to believe that a stock can or should do better than expected, we then make a judgment as to whether the reward-to-risk ratio justifies getting involved.

We also seek companies that pay high dividends, typically two to three times higher, as a percentage of their price, than the market averages. We also look for companies that trade at lower earnings or have book values higher than the average stock of their type in the market. We call this form of equity investing "high-yield value, with a catalyst."

To date, we have been sticking to only mid- to large-cap US listed stocks that pay qualified dividends, which are taxed at lower rates than vehicles such as REITs, MLPs, or BDCs. We also do not invest in tobacco stocks due to the legal and legislative risks inherent in those companies.

Most high-dividend common stocks are considered value stocks, meaning they have lower price-to-earnings ratios than the market averages, and therefore tend to yield more than similar company stocks. This is a convoluted way of saying that value stocks are cheap because they have something wrong with them, which causes them to be judged less attractive than the alternatives. Thus, the stocks we invest in are probably not in favor and have zero or negative price momentum when we first buy them because they are thought to have problems. The good news is that most of them have problems we think can be fixed, at which time they should be reappraised at a higher value.

WHAT SUPPRESSES A STOCK'S VALUE?

The fact is, most stocks whose prices are suppressed are down for valid reasons. These reasons could include:

Maturity—The value might be suppressed because there is a consensus that the company is at the mature end of its life cycle and about to go into decline. Not surprisingly, most high-dividend-paying companies are indeed in the mature part of their life cycle, which is why investors see more value in receiving dividends than in having the profits reinvested in the company for future growth.

A Traumatic Event—Another reason the price could be suppressed is due to a traumatic market event that affects a particular sector. The COVID-19 pandemic in 2020 shut down large swaths of the economy for eighteen months. The regional banking crisis in the spring of 2023[72] prompted by the Fed's aggressive interest rate hikes caused two banks to fail and put many more at risk. Those are just two examples.

Underestimated Potential—A stock's value could also be suppressed just because the market doesn't fully realize the potential the company has for strategic growth initiatives, such as mergers and acquisitions.

Business Cycles—Or the company could be cyclical by nature and, if the economy is slowing, the sentiment pendulum may lead investors to over-discount the likely decline, so that investing for the rebound offers outsized returns.

Given all these factors, an investor who chooses individual high-dividend-value-based stocks must do more research than the typical growth-only investor in order to get it right. This multileveled evaluation isn't just based on hard data research; it is also based on how the data is interpreted. For every high-dividend, value-based investor who thinks a particular undervalued stock has upside potential, there is an investor on the other side of the trade who believes the stock is undervalued for a legitimate reason. Both may agree on the facts, but they have different time horizons or predictions.

In order to develop informed opinions without crossing the line into obtaining insider information, good equity investors must read reports and journals by parties who both support and oppose their opinion. They must also constantly cultivate relationships with Wall Street analysts and consultants to get their views and try to determine the truth about each company and to separate facts from opinions.

After fully digesting all the information on a prospective investment, a good analyst or portfolio manager will then typically create a list of questions and put them to the company, its peers, and other stakeholders. The short-term goal is to get a variety of answers to the same set of questions, knowing that there will be conflicts and widely differing views. The middle-term goal is to form an opinion about whether management is honest and capable of delivering on their goals to improve the company; in other words, to determine if a stock is cheap and out of favor for a good reason that can't be fixed, or if it is undervalued due to a circumstance that can improve, and therefore has a hidden value that most analysts and investors don't realize.

LEGITIMATE, STRATEGIC INVESTING

But the process usually doesn't end there either, as more questions will often arise that require more back-and-forth between the investor, the company, its competitors, and other analysts. The point is that this type of investing demands a very engaged and rigorous effort, which makes it as far removed from mere gambling as you can possibly get! This kind of fundamental research is also much more strategic than just looking at financials, technical data, and market sentiment. This type of investing is about truly understanding the structure of the company, where the risks are hidden, and where the opportunities can be found.

And even after all of this work, the best investors only get it right 65 percent of the time. But that is usually enough for the portfolio to outshine the alternatives, and with less risk. In narrow markets, like the "Magnificent Seven" technology rally in 2023,[73] or the FAANG surge in 2019, high-dividend-value stocks may not have underperformed these rallies on a price appreciation basis, but they paid out higher yields.

So, even when these rigorous analysts and portfolio managers underperform their high-growth alternatives, or get their stock predictions wrong temporarily, at least they are collecting a dividend return for their clients. In our case, oftentimes this return is in the range of 4 percent or so, which—again—is income the client can spend or reinvest, depending on their needs, without having to sell the stock and potentially pay capital gains tax.

As discussed earlier, whenever you reinvest dividends (or interest payments) received in a down market, you are "reloading the spring" so that when the stock does eventually recover, your portfolio will recover faster. So, even if it takes some time before a stock's hidden value gets triggered, this strategy can be highly effective thanks to the intensive research and active management that goes into it, and the constant stream of cash flows that come out of it. Simply put, you're much more of a legitimate investor with a dividend strategy than you are when investing in growth-only stocks!

CHAPTER 9

OUR BIG FAT HAIRY AUDACIOUS GOAL

I mentioned this briefly in the first chapter, but prior to entering college, I had a conversation with my high school guidance counselor about a serious concern of mine. I learned pretty early on in high school that I hated writing, and anytime a teacher assigned an essay, whether it was two paragraphs or ten pages, the result was the same. I'd put it off until the last minute because I had zero interest in doing it. So, I asked my guidance counselor what major I could select in college that all but guaranteed I would never have to write a single essay. And that's the story of how I came to be a math major.

It took me about six months to put this book together, and it was a long, arduous six months. I feel the same way about writing in my fifties as I did as a teenager. But those six months were nothing compared to the twenty-plus years I've spent fighting tooth and nail against the financial establishment to try to bring some financial sanity to this great country.

When I made the leap into the world of investing for income in 1999, lots of people thought I was crazy. Why would I bother with anything else when growth was so hot? The answer soon became clear. The market crashed. And in a financially coherent world, you might think or at least hope that would be the end of the story. You would think that people would have wised up. When the market crashed in 2000 and my clients were mostly safe, I certainly felt like I had won some all-important debate and I could put the issue to rest. But I never imagined just how deeply entrenched the idea of getting rich in the stock market had become in our culture. I don't delude myself for a moment (and I don't think anyone does) that everyone gets to be rich. We all get our shot, and some make it, some don't, and that's OK. You don't have to be rich to lead a happy life. Gallup reported in 2011 that our happiness peaks at a certain income level (which was $75,000 at the time), and that any amount over that doesn't really lead to a significant improvement in our overall quality of life.[74]

So, again, I don't think everyone gets or even needs to be rich, but I do believe that those who work hard should be able to afford a decent life for themselves. And I believe that if you work hard your entire life, you shouldn't have to work hard in retirement.

That's why I created Retirement Income Source. At the end of the day, retirees need income first and growth second, because if they keep relying on growth to get their "income," that money won't be there when the market takes another dive, and that's when they'll need it most. We tend to think that the older we get, the less money we need, but the opposite is really the case. The more you age, the more money you need. Inflation, growing healthcare costs, and growing life spans are just three reasons why. There are psychological reasons, too. No one wants to watch their precious nest egg dwindle the older and more frail they get. Investing for income is all about keeping your security blanket so you can live the lifestyle you want without having to worry about it.

MY MISSION

Seventeen years ago, I realized that my influence as an independent advisor could only reach so far. That's why I founded Advisors' Academy in 2006 so I could reach more people. Advisors' Academy[75] is a network of financial advisors all over the nation who have made it their fiduciary responsibility to reposition their clients' portfolios in a way that will help them generate income during retirement, while avoiding the risks that come with secular bear markets.

It was a step in the right direction. However, after some time, I realized I needed to do more. For the next eight years, I saw some success with Advisors' Academy, convincing dozens of financial advisors across the country that they needed to adopt an income-focused retirement strategy for their clients who were at or near retirement age. But what I quickly realized is that most financial advisors are unsure how to invest their clients' money without resorting to the same, outdated strategies, such as the growth stock model.

That's one reason I founded Sound Income Strategies[76] in 2014, a registered investment advisory firm that equips our network of financial advisors with the precise strategies they need to invest their clients' money. Through Sound Income Strategies, we are able to generate income in the form of interest and dividends for our clients, allowing them to live solely off the income their investments generate without ever touching their principal, and thereby preserving their nest egg.

Now, I've gone one step further by launching our most ambitious project: Retirement Income Source. Just as department stores popped up to meet the consumer demands of a growing population, the purpose of Retirement Income Source is to meet the investment demands of a population that needs income to last their entire lifetime with less risk.

STARING DOWN THE BARREL OF A GUN

The problem we have right now is that, as members of the Income Generation, we are at a crossroads. Although most of us have probably saved enough to retire, we haven't saved enough to survive another devastating market crash like those we saw in 2000 and 2008.

Unfortunately, I think the likelihood of us avoiding another crash of that magnitude is unlikely, especially considering the drastic actions our central banks have taken to get the economy moving after the financial crisis, the financial engineering corporations have used to inflate their stock prices, and our historically high levels of debt.

That's why I'm aggressively pushing Retirement Income Source forward. Our "big, fat, hairy audacious goal is to reach seven out of every ten baby boomers" with our message.

This is a very ambitious and, I believe, very important project. Until recently, most investors simply didn't have the right alternatives when it comes to investing their money. That's why so many people are willing to accept the risk of investing in growth stocks, unaware of the vast opportunities in alternative investment strategies and the advisors who specialize in them. To be sure, that pool of advisors is limited, which is why I'm fighting hard against the financial establishment to build out a national infrastructure dedicated to Income Specialists through Retirement Income Source.

When you boil it all down, the average financial advisor is chasing after the people with a lot of zeros at the end of their bank account. That leaves fewer and fewer advisors left over for the rest of the population, and fewer still who are comfortable wading into the pool of dividend stocks, bonds, and bond-like instruments.

That's why my mission is to provide an income solution for the average investor. And rather than settle for average results, we're discarding this notion that "you get what you pay for" by providing institutional-style investing (the kind Wall Street provides to its wealthiest clients) to everyday investors just like you.

Except instead of focusing on the "Growth," we're focusing on the "Income." And instead of charging the typical Wall Street fees, we're doing it for a price that's affordable for anyone.

WHY NOW?

The question you might have is: Why has no one else tried to do something like this? With such a large vacuum in the financial industry for folks who want a reasonable rate of return with less risk, why has no one tried to carve out their niche in the industry as I have?

The reason is that it's extremely hard to do on a large scale.

For one thing, there's more money in this industry for growth-based advisors than there is for income-based advisors. Since there's a higher potential return with investing for growth, there are higher fees. And since growth advisors get paid more often in fees, there are more advisors who want to go that route.

Secondly, growth advisors attract higher-net-worth clients. That's because they can promise the potential for higher returns. Since every advisor wants to catch the big fish client, there are more advisors chasing after them than there are advisors chasing everyday clients.

Finally, very few people understand the complex rules of investing in high-dividend stocks or individual bonds and bond-like investments. Most of the advisors working today got their start during the 1980s and 1990s bull market when growth was the only game in town.

I've personally been dedicated to the world of income-generating investments for the last twenty-five years. I started from my office in Westbrook, Connecticut, and began doing educational workshops all over the state. But I eventually had to come to terms with the fact that I could only do so much good on my own.

I realized I had to build a larger network of advisors if my message was to make any sort of significant impact.

Again, that's when I launched Advisors' Academy, which was a step in the right direction. Today, Advisors' Academy is thriving, with advisors across the country, many of whom are media names in their own right. We are all just as committed to getting this message of income out to the world today as we were way back in 2006 when the Academy first started. There is still a lot of work to do. It's an ongoing fight for several reasons.

One is that people simply don't like change. Another is that dividend stocks and bonds aren't sexy. They're not as easy to sell. Folks don't get how they work. They're too hard to invest in. Plus, as mentioned, there's not as much money in it for the advisor. And it requires a certain level of expertise, resources, and personnel that most small advisory offices simply aren't equipped to take on.

And that, once again, is one of the main reasons I launched Sound Income Strategies in 2014, so that the advisors network I'd established through Advisors' Academy could focus on spreading the message while my internal team handled the day-to-day task of portfolio management. We would invest their clients' money for them, and we did it for less than they'd get charged by a typical advisor who put their money in growth-only strategies.

With this approach, we were able to bring more and more advisors into our fold. But there was still one big problem.

Most advisors still didn't want to make the switch because, no matter how you slice it, there's more money in growth than there is in income.

So, what do you do about that?

The answer is, you go direct. You go to the consumer.

SPREADING THE WORD

I've been doing this for years now with my TV and radio show, Retirement Income Source with David J. Scranton, where I've been fortunate to speak with some of the most important financial minds of our time. People like Jim Rogers,[77] Robert J. Shiller,[78] Mark Faber,[79] Steve Forbes, Jr.,[80] Peter Schiff,[81] Dan Gainor,[82] George Gilder,[83] and many more.

I brought these people on my show to talk about issues facing the Income Generation right now. I wanted to do more than just educate; I wanted to provide the solution. Through Retirement Income Source, I'm now able to do that on a much larger scale.

For the last twenty-five years, I've been creating an infrastructure so the members of the Income Generation can get exposure to the types of investments that offer better protection, and a reasonable rate of return in the form of income.

Again, we're talking about institutional-style investing, the kind you normally have to have millions of dollars to get access to. We literally have several analysts whose sole job it is to sit in front of a computer all day monitoring Bloomberg Terminals for swap opportunities in high-dividend stocks and in the bond market that require you to be able to pounce on them in a moment's notice.

That's what we offer in a nutshell.

And as difficult as it might seem to believe, it's completely revolutionary. No one to my knowledge has done anything on this kind of scale.

IT'S TIME TO MAKE THE SWITCH

They say the worst impediment to overcoming addiction and staying in recovery is being overexposed to the drug you're addicted to. That's a problem our generation is faced with every day.

We've all heard stories about people who bought growth stocks that doubled or tripled. Perhaps that's happened to you on a few occasions. When that happens, it's like winning the lottery. And as we've discussed, there isn't much of a difference between hitting the slots and speculating in the market; it's gambling. When your money doubles, it feels like the jackpot. I get how addiction works, but eventually, we all have to come to terms with our addiction. If we forget the lessons we learned from Enron[84] and WorldCom,[85] you know what they say: those who forget history are doomed to repeat it.

That's why I'm working to build out a national infrastructure for income seekers and income advisors through Retirement Income Source. I want people to have the best retirement they can possibly have—and that's why I'm bringing Retirement Income Source directly to you.

LOOK OUT FOR A RETIREMENT INCOME SOURCE NEAR YOU

I'm confident that, after reading everything, you'll see the benefit of investing in the "I" and not the "G" much more clearly than any advisor who's still stuck in the 1990s mentally and addicted to growth-only investing. It's time that we, together, create a new financial establishment that caters to middle America and not the 1 percent. It's time we get back to the basics and invest the way our parents did before we all got caught up in the financial insanity of the 1980s and 1990s bull market.

That's our goal with Retirement Income Source: to create a new standard by which clients come together to hold their financial advisors accountable. I've franchised Retirement Income Source so that any income specialist can call us up and brand themselves with our message so prospective clients know they mean business and know that they're going to invest their money the right way.

I don't pretend for a moment that this book has completely persuaded you to reposition your financial life according to our model. My only hope is that you'll take what I've said to heart and at least start a conversation about it. If nothing else, I hope this book inspires you to head over to www.retirementincomesource.com to find a Retirement Income Source in your area and at least have a conversation.

Go in with no expectations, have a conversation with one of our trusted advisors, and see what you think. If you like the idea of keeping the money you've worked so hard to accumulate, if you like the idea of sidestepping the next market crash, if you like the idea of stable returns in an otherwise unstable market, then I ask you to have an open mind. I ask you to share our story with others. And I ask you to do everything within your power to create for yourself the retirement that you deserve.

AUTHOR BIO

David J. Scranton, CFA®, CFP®, ChFC®, CLU®, is an Amazon best-selling author, nationally recognized money manager, and founder of Sound Income Group, Sound Income Strategies, Retirement Income Source, and Advisors' Academy. David is on a mission to help retirees and pre-retirees understand the strategic value of shifting their investment focus to an income-first approach.

David has spent more than three decades in the financial services industry, with most of that time spent specializing in income-generating investments. In 1999, he made the switch to an income-first approach for his clients, while many of his Wall Street contemporaries continued to focus on growth in the stock market. As a result, he was able to help many of his clients avoid damaging losses during the major market corrections that began in 2000 and again in 2008.

Knowing the market chaos of the early-to-mid 2000s was only the beginning of this new age of uncertainty, David launched a plan to reach investors nationwide with his message about the value of investing for income. That plan led to the founding of Advisors' Academy, through which David recruited like-minded advisors nationwide and coached them in his methods. From there, he launched Sound Income Strategies, a Registered Investment Advisory and money management firm specializing in actively managed fixed-income strategies, followed by Retirement Income Source, a national franchise of fiduciary Income Specialists.

A highly sought-after industry thought leader, David regularly shares his market insights on networks such as Fox Business, CNBC, and Bloomberg. He has his own radio show, "Retirement Income Source," which airs weekly on stations nationwide. He also hosts the popular "Retirement Income Source" YouTube channel to help educate viewers about financial issues that could impact their retirement. In addition to *Retirement Income Source: The Ultimate Guide to Eternal Income*, David is also the author of the Amazon bestseller, *Return on Principle*.

NOTES

1. Google LLC: Was founded in 1998 by Larry Page and Sergey Brin while they were PhD students at Stanford University in California. Together they own about 14 percent of its shares and control 56 percent of the stockholder voting power through super voting stock. They incorporated Google as a privately held company on September 4, 1998. An initial public offering (IPO) took place on August 19, 2004, and Google moved to its headquarters in Mountain View, California, nicknamed the Googleplex. In August 2015, Google announced plans to reorganize its various interests as a conglomerate called Alphabet Inc. Google is Alphabet's leading subsidiary and will continue to be the umbrella company for Alphabet's internet interests. Sundar Pichai was appointed CEO of Google, replacing Larry Page who became the CEO of Alphabet.

   https://en.wikipedia.org/wiki/Google

2. Dot-com bubble: Also known as the dot-com boom, the tech bubble, and the internet bubble; was a historic speculative bubble and period of excessive speculation mainly in the United States that occurred roughly from 1995 to 2000, a period of extreme growth in the use and adoption of the internet. The Nasdaq Composite stock market index, which included many internet-based companies, peaked in value on March 10, 2000, before crashing. The burst of the bubble, known as the dot-com crash, lasted from March 11, 2000, to October 9, 2002.

https://en.wikipedia.org/wiki/Dot-com_bubble

Financial crisis of 2007–2008: The 2007–2008 financial crisis, or Global Financial Crisis, was the most severe worldwide economic crisis since the Great Depression. Predatory lending in the form of subprime mortgages targeting low-income homebuyers, excessive risk-taking by global financial institutions, a continuous buildup of toxic assets within banks, and the bursting of the US housing bubble culminated in a "perfect storm," which led to the Great Recession.

https://en.wikipedia.org/wiki/2007%E2%80%932008_financial_crisis

3. Macrotrends. Dow Jones—DJIA—100 Year Historical Chart. Interactive chart of the Dow Jones Industrial Average (DJIA) stock market index for the last one hundred years. Historical data is inflation-adjusted using the headline CPI and each data point represents the month-end closing value. The current month is updated on an hourly basis with today's latest value.

https://www.macrotrends.net/1319/dow-jones-100-year-historical-chart

4. The Income Generation: Sound Income Strategies was founded by David Scranton (CLU, ChFC, CFP®, CFA, MSFS). Dave has gained much notoriety during his thirty years in the industry as an advisor who is particularly protective of his clients' assets. For the past twenty years, he has specialized in the universe of income-generating savings and investment strategies. Sound Income Strategies is a registered investment advisory firm specializing in the active management of income-generating portfolios. With our years of industry experience, we focus on maximizing the value of your income portfolio and help you build a retirement plan that delivers dependable income, growth potential, and, most importantly, defense against damaging losses. As a registered investment advisory firm, we honor our fiduciary respon-

sibility. As spelled out in the US Investment Advisers Act of 1940, our goal is to always act and serve in the best interest of our clients.

http://theincomegeneration.com/

5. Federal Reserve: The Federal Reserve System is the central bank of the United States. It performs five general functions to promote the effective operation of the US economy and, more generally, the public interest. The Federal Reserve:

- Conducts the nation's monetary policy to promote maximum employment, stable prices, and moderate long-term interest rates in the US economy.

- Promotes the stability of the financial system and seeks to minimize and contain systemic risks through active monitoring and engagement in the United States and abroad.

- Promotes the safety and soundness of individual financial institutions and monitors their impact on the financial system as a whole.

https://www.federalreserve.gov/aboutthefed/files/pf_1.pdf

6. *LIFE* magazine: Was an American magazine published weekly until 1972, as an intermittent "special" until 1978, and as a monthly from 1978 to 2000. During its golden age from 1936 to 1972, Life was a wide-ranging weekly general interest magazine known for the quality of its photography.

https://en.wikipedia.org/wiki/Life_(magazine)

7. Industrial Revolution: In modern history, the process of change from an agrarian and handicraft economy to one dominated by industry and machine manufacturing. This process began in Britain in the eighteenth century and from there spread to other parts of the world. Although used earlier by French writers, the term Industrial Revolution was first popularized by the English economic historian Arnold

Toynbee (1852–1883) to describe Britain's economic development from 1760 to 1840. Since Toynbee's time, the term has been more broadly applied.

https://www.britannica.com/event/Industrial-Revolution

8. Macy's: No one would have guessed that the small, fancy dry goods store that opened on the corner of 14th Street and 6th Avenue in New York City in 1858 would grow to be one of the largest retailers in the world. But after several failed retail ventures, Rowland Hussey Macy's determination and ingenuity paid off at the age of thirty-six with the launch of R.H. Macy & Co. He adopted a red star as his symbol of success, dating back to his days as a sailor. By 1877, R.H. Macy & Co. had become a full-fledged department store occupying the ground space of eleven adjacent buildings.

https://www.macysinc.com/company/about/default.aspx

9. Marshall Field & Company: Traces its antecedents to a dry goods store opened at 137 Lake Street in Chicago, Illinois, in 1852 by Potter Palmer (1826–1902), eponymously named P. Palmer & Company. In 1856, twenty-one-year-old Marshall Field (1834–1906) moved to the booming Midwestern city of Chicago on the southwest shores of Lake Michigan from Pittsfield, Massachusetts, and found work at the city's then-largest dry goods firm—Cooley, Wadsworth & Company.

http://www.encyclopedia.chicagohistory.org/pages/2663.html

10. Retirement Income Source: Retirement Income Source is comprised of a network of franchised financial advisors specializing in income-generating investment strategies designed to preserve client assets and provide income through interest and dividend return. Retirement Income Source is a subsidiary of Sound Income Group.

https://retirementincomesource.com/

NOTES

11. Albert Einstein (March 14, 1879, to April 18, 1955): Was a German mathematician and physicist who developed the special and general theories of relativity.

    https://www.biography.com/people/albert-einstein-9285408

12. Bristol, Connecticut: Is a suburban city located in Hartford County, Connecticut, United States, 20 miles (32 km) southwest of Hartford. The city is also 120 miles southwest of Boston, and approximately 100 miles northeast of New York City. As of the 2010 census, the population of the city was 60,477.

    https://en.wikipedia.org/wiki/Bristol,_Connecticut

13. Otto Eduard Leopold von Bismarck was a Prussian and later German statesman and diplomat. From his origins in the upper class of Junker landowners, Bismarck rose rapidly in Prussian politics, and from 1862 to 1890 he was the minister president and foreign minister of Prussia.

    https://en.wikipedia.org/wiki/Otto_von_Bismarck

14. Ida May Fuller: Miss Fuller filed her retirement claim on November 4, 1939, having worked under Social Security for a little short of three years. While running an errand she dropped by the Rutland Social Security office to ask about possible benefits. She would later observe: "It wasn't that I expected anything, mind you, but I knew I'd been paying for something called Social Security and I wanted to ask the people in Rutland about it." Her claim was taken by Claims Clerk Elizabeth Corcoran Burke and transmitted to the Claims Division in Washington, DC, for adjudication. The case was adjudicated and reviewed and sent to the Treasury Department for payment in January 1940.

    https://en.wikipedia.org/wiki/Ida_May_Fuller

15. US Bureau of Labor Statistics: Data dated 2022, Stated that the average hours per day spent watching TV for ages fifteen years and over was 2.8 hours. The average retiree ages sixty-five and over watched 4.38 hours per day. Those fifty-five to sixty-four years on average tuned in for about 3.23 hours.

    https://www.bls.gov/news.release/pdf/atus.pdf

16. Lump-Sum Purchase: A lump-sum purchase, also known as a basket purchase, occurs when a company or an individual buys multiple assets together for one single, combined price. This kind of purchase often happens when buying a business, where the price paid is for a combination of assets such as buildings, land, equipment, and inventory.

    https://www.superfastcpa.com/what-is-a-lump-sum-purchase/#:~:text=A%20lump%2Dsum%20purchase%2C%20also,for%20one%20single%2C%20combined%20price.

17. Current US Inflation Rates: 2000–2024: The annual inflation rate for the United States was 3.1 percent for the twelve months ending January, compared to the previous rate of 3.4 percent, according to US Labor Department data published on February 13, 2024.

    https://www.usinflationcalculator.com/inflation/current-inflation-rates/

18. Federal Reserve Bank of St. Louis: Healthy Inflation? Inflation in the healthcare industry versus general CPI. Some components of the consumer price index have consistently, over several decades, risen faster than the rest.

    https://fredblog.stlouisfed.org/2017/07/healthy-inflation/

19. Medicare Part B: You pay a premium each month for Part B. Your Part B premium will be automatically deducted from your benefit payment if you get benefits from one of these:

NOTES

- Social Security
- Railroad Retirement Board
- Office of Personnel Management

If you don't get these benefit payments, you'll get a bill.

Most people will pay the standard premium amount. If your modified adjusted gross income is above a certain amount, you may pay an Income-Related Monthly Adjustment Amount (IRMAA). Medicare uses the modified adjusted gross income reported on your IRS tax return from two years ago. This is the most recent tax return information provided to Social Security by the IRS.

https://www.medicare.gov/your-medicare-costs/part-b-costs

20. The 4 percent rule: Is often confused with the Multiply by 25 Rule, for obvious reasons—the 4 percent rule, as its name implies, also assumes a 4 percent return. The 4 percent rule, however, guides how much you should withdraw annually once you're retired. As the name implies, this rule of thumb says you should withdraw 4 percent of your retirement portfolio the first year.

    https://www.thebalance.com/
    dont-confuse-these-two-retirement-rules-of-thumb-453920

21. IRA Traditional and Roth IRAs: For both traditional and Roth IRAs you can contribute up to $7,000 for 2024, up from $6,500 in 2023. Retirement savers age fifty and older can chip in an extra $1,000 a year as a catch-up contribution, so $8,000 in all.

    https://www.aarp.org/retirement/planning-for-retirement/info-2023/
    ira-contribution-limits.html?cmp=KNC-DSO-COR-Core-Retirement-NonBrand-Exact-51112-GOOG-RETIREMENT-Contribution-Exact-NonBrand&gad_source=1&gclid=EAIaIQobChMIgJmq
    obCrhAMVeIFaBR3ZFASiEAAYASAAEgJ6tvD_BwE&gclsrc=aw.ds

22. Monte Carlo Methods: A broad class of computational algorithms that rely on repeated random sampling to obtain numerical results. Their essential idea is using randomness to solve problems that might be deterministic in principle. They are often used in physical and mathematical problems and are most useful when it is difficult or impossible to use other approaches. Monte Carlo methods are mainly used in three problem classes: optimization, numerical integration, and generating draws from a probability distribution.

    https://en.wikipedia.org/wiki/Monte_Carlo_method

23. Russian Roulette: Is a lethal game of chance in which a player places a single round in a revolver, spins the cylinder, places the muzzle against their head, and pulls the trigger. Russian refers to the supposed country of origin, and roulette to the element of risk-taking and the spinning of the revolver's cylinder, which is reminiscent of a spinning roulette wheel.

    https://en.wikipedia.org/wiki/Russian_roulette

24. Vanguard. "When Inflation Volatility Spikes: Setting a Realistic Withdrawal Rate," April 12, 2022. "Philadelphia Federal Reserve's 10-year projections for higher inflation and moderate to low returns for both stocks and bonds, forecasts the sustainable inflation-adjusted annual withdrawal rate to be between 2.8% and 3.3%."

    https://corporate.vanguard.com/content/corporatesite/us/en/corp/articles/when-inflation-volatility-spikes.html

25. Dollar Cost Averaging: Dollar cost averaging is the strategy of spreading out your stock or fund purchases, buying at regular intervals and in roughly equal amounts. So instead of buying stock in a single large purchase, you invest that same amount over a year or two years or even indefinitely, by regularly adding money to the market.

    When done properly, dollar cost averaging can have significant benefits for your portfolio. This is because the strategy "smooths" your purchase

NOTES

price over time and helps ensure that you're not dumping all your money in at a high point for prices.

Dollar cost averaging can be especially powerful in a bear market, allowing you to "buy the dips," or purchase stock at low points when most investors are too afraid to buy. Committing to this strategy means that you will be investing when the market or a stock is down, and that's when investors score the best deals.

https://www.nerdwallet.com/blog/investing/dollar-cost-averaging-2/

26. Reverse Dollar Cost Averaging: Reverse dollar cost averaging is the opposite of dollar cost averaging—taking the same amount of money out of investments at regular intervals. For retirees, you'll likely need to withdraw from investments regularly to cover monthly expenses.

    https://www.pathfinderfinancial.com/blog-01/risk-reverse-dollar-cost-averaging-retirees#:~:text=Reverse%20dollar%2Dcost%20averaging%20is,regularly%20to%20cover%20monthly%20expenses

27. Patrick Peason: Has been in the financial services industry for thirty-one years and specializes in the unique challenges facing today's retirees and pre-retirees. In today's tough market economy, seniors need to fully understand all the various options that are currently available to assist them in protecting and growing their investment portfolios.

    https://peasongroup.com/our-team/

28. The American Institute of CPAs: As the national, professional organization for all Certified Public Accountants, the AICPA's mission is to power the success of global business, CPAs, CGMAs, and specialty credentials by providing the most relevant knowledge, resources and advocacy, and protecting the evolving public interest. From financial literacy to public policy issues and peer review transparency to audit committee effectiveness, the AICPA is working to ensure that the

public remains confident in the integrity, objectivity, competence, and professionalism of CPAs.

https://www.aicpa.org/forthepublic.html

29. Standard & Poor's 500 Index Fund: Picking a fund that tracks the S&P 500 Index may seem like a simple task. After all, an index fund is designed to mirror an index's holdings, so issues such as a manager's quality or investment style don't come into play.

But it's actually harder than you might expect. There are more than 50 S&P 500 Index funds to choose from.

https://www.consumerreports.org/personal-investing/how-to-choose-an-index-fund/

30. FanDuel: Is a daily fantasy sports provider from the United States and bookmaker based in New York City. Originally founded in 2009, the service is the second largest DFS service in the country (behind DraftKings) based on entry fees and user base.

https://en.wikipedia.org/wiki/FanDuel

31. Warren Buffett: Born August 30, 1930, is an American business magnate, investor, speaker, and philanthropist who serves as the chairman and CEO of Berkshire Hathaway. He is considered one of the most successful investors in the world and has a net worth of US $122 billion as of January 2024, making him the third wealthiest person in the world.

https://en.wikipedia.org/wiki/Warren_Buffett

32. Long-Term Average Market Return: The stock market has historically returned an average of 10 percent annually. Over nearly the last century, the stock market's average return is about 10 percent annually. That's what long-term investors in the stock market can expect to earn if they use the stock market model for their investments over time.

https://www.nerdwallet.com/blog/investing/average-stock-market-return/

33. Long-Term Growth Rate LTG: Is an investing strategy and concept in which a security appreciates in value for a relatively long period of time, whether or not this growth begins immediately or develops gradually. Long-term growth is a relative term as investors' time horizons differ, based on their individual styles.

    https://www.investopedia.com/terms/l/longtermgrowth.asp

34. Tech Bubble: The bubble popping in 2000 (it was not 2001) was a lot like an avalanche. It wasn't clear exactly which snowflake was the one that put it over the tipping point, but once confidence was lost, it went very quickly.

    https://www.quora.com/What-was-the-trigger-for-the-tech-bubble-to-burst-in-2000

35. A Secular Bear Market: Is categorized by below average stock market returns over a period of nearly a generation, while a cyclical bull market's average length approximates that of a business cycle. Since hitting bottom in March 2009, equities have enjoyed a nearly four-year cyclical bull market. The only question on every investor's mind should now be: is this the beginning of a new secular trend? Or, simply a cyclical divergence within a secular bear market?

    https://seekingalpha.com/article/1097631-on-secular-vs-cyclical-bull-and-bear-markets

36. Bear-Market Cycle: Just like a secular bull market, a secular bear market is one that lasts between five and twenty-five years. And while the average length of a secular bear market is about seventeen years, there may be smaller bull or bear markets within it. Still, the average bear market is much shorter—usually under a year—and so definitions of what constitutes a secular bear market vary.

RETIREMENT INCOME SOURCE

https://www.thestreet.com/markets/what-is-a-bear-market-14713949

37. COVID-19 Pandemic: The global COVID-19 pandemic hit the United States in March 2020. It has had far-reaching economic consequences, including the COVID-19 Recession, the second largest global recession in recent history, decreased business in the services sector during the COVID-19 lockdowns, the 2020 stock market crash, which included the largest single-week stock market decline since the financial crisis of 2007–08. It led to governments providing an unprecedented amount of stimulus.

https://en.wikipedia.org/wiki/Economic_impact_of_the_COVID-19_pandemic

38. Dividend Stocks: Dividend stocks are companies that pay out regular dividends. Dividend stocks are usually well-established companies with a track record of distributing earnings back to shareholders.

https://www.investopedia.com/dividend-stocks-4689744

39. Investment Bonds: Bonds, also known as fixed-income instruments, are used by governments or companies to raise money by borrowing from investors. Bonds are typically issued to raise funds for specific projects. In return, the bond issuer promises to pay back the investment, with interest, over a certain period of time.

https://www.blackrock.com/us/individual/education/how-to-invest-in-bonds#:~:text=Bonds%20%E2%80%93%20also%20known%20as%20fixed,a%20certain%20period%20of%20time

40. Ben Shalom Bernanke: Born December 13, 1953, is an American economist at the Brookings Institution who served two terms as chair of the Federal Reserve, the central bank of the United States, from 2006 to 2014. During his tenure as chair, Bernanke oversaw the Federal Reserve's response to the late-2000s financial crisis.

https://en.wikipedia.org/wiki/Ben_Bernanke

41. Quantitative Easing: Also known as large-scale asset purchases, is an expansionary monetary policy whereby a central bank buys predetermined amounts of government bonds or other financial assets in order to stimulate the economy and increase liquidity. An unconventional form of monetary policy, it is usually used when inflation is very low or negative, and standard expansionary monetary policy has become ineffective.

    https://en.wikipedia.org/wiki/Quantitative_easing

42. Central Banks: Reserve bank or monetary authority is the institution that manages the currency, money supply, and interest rates of a state or formal monetary union and oversees their commercial banking system. In contrast to a commercial bank, a central bank possesses a monopoly on increasing the monetary base in the state, and also generally controls the printing/coining of the national currency, which serves as the state's legal tender. A central bank also acts as a lender of last resort to the banking sector during times of financial crisis. Most central banks also have supervisory and regulatory powers.

    https://en.wikipedia.org/wiki/Central_bank

43. Operation Twist: The Federal Open Market Committee action known as Operation Twist (named for the twist dance craze of the time) began in 1961. The intent was to flatten the yield curve in order to promote capital inflows and strengthen the dollar. The Fed utilized open market operations to shorten the maturity of public debt in the open market. It performed the "twist" by selling some of the short-term debt (with three years or less to maturity) it purchased as part of the quantitative easing policy back into the market and using the money received from this to buy longer term government debt. Although this action was marginally successful in reducing the spread between long-term maturities and short-term maturities, Vincent Reinhart and others have suggested it did not continue for a sufficient period of time to be effective.

https://en.wikipedia.org/wiki/History_of_Federal_Open_Market_Committee_actions#Operation_Twist_(1961)

44. Nasdaq: Is an American stock exchange. It is the second largest stock exchange in the world by market capitalization, behind only the New York Stock Exchange located in the same city. The exchange platform is owned by NASDAQ, Inc., which also owns the Nasdaq Nordic (formerly known as OMX) and Nasdaq Baltic stock market network and several US stock and options exchanges.

    https://en.wikipedia.org/wiki/NASDAQ

45. Apple Inc.: Apple Computers, Inc. was founded on April 1, 1976, by college dropouts Steve Jobs and Steve Wozniak, who brought to the new company a vision of changing the way people viewed computers. Jobs and Wozniak wanted to make computers small enough for people to have them in their homes or offices. Simply put, they wanted a computer that was user-friendly.

    https://www.loc.gov/rr/business/businesshistory/April/apple.html

46. Wall Street Journal. "Corporate Stock Buybacks Help Keep Market Afloat," February 27, 2023. "Companies on the S&P 500 have poured more than $5.3 trillion into repurchasing their own shares. WSJ explains how stock buybacks work."

    https://www.wsj.com/articles/corporate-stock-buybacks-help-keep-market-afloat-67f95615

47. CRSP: The Center for Research in Security Prices, LLC is a provider of historical stock market and investable index data. CRSP is an affiliate of the Booth School of Business at the University of Chicago. CRSP maintains some of the largest and most comprehensive proprietary historical databases in stock market research.

    https://en.wikipedia.org/wiki/Center_for_Research_in_Security_Prices

48. Index Funds: An "index fund" is a type of mutual fund or exchange-traded fund that seeks to track the returns of a market index. The S&P 500 Index, the Russell 2000 Index, and the Wilshire 5000 Total Market Index are just a few examples of market indexes that index funds may seek to track. A market index measures the performance of a "basket" of securities (like stocks or bonds), which is meant to represent a sector of a stock market, or of an economy. You cannot invest directly in a market index, but because index funds track a market index they provide an indirect investment option.

    https://www.investor.gov/introduction-investing/investing-basics/investment-products/mutual-funds-and-exchange-traded-4

49. Algorithmic Trading: Algorithmic trading is a method of executing orders using automated preprogrammed trading instructions accounting for variables such as time, price, and volume. This type of trading attempts to leverage the speed and computational resources of computers relative to human traders.

    https://en.wikipedia.org/wiki/Algorithmic_trading

50. Benzinga. "What Percentage of Stock Trades Are Made by Bots and Algorithms?" June 14, 2023. "Algorithmic trading, which relies heavily on programmed instructions, already dominates global markets. It accounts for 60%-73% of equities trading on US markets, 60% in Europe and 45% in the Asia-Pacific, according to Select USA."

    https://www.benzinga.com/general/topics/23/06/32861724/what-percentage-of-stock-trades-are-made-by-bots-and-algorithms

51. Dodd-Frank Wall Street Reform and Consumer Protection Act: The Dodd-Frank Wall Street Reform and Consumer Protection Act is legislation that was passed by the US Congress in response to financial industry behavior that led to the financial crisis of 2007–08. It sought to make the US financial system safer for consumers and taxpayers. Named for sponsors Sen. Christopher J. Dodd (D-Conn.) and Rep. Barney Frank (D-Mass.), the act contains numerous provisions, spelled

out over 848 pages, that were to be implemented over a period of several years.

https://www.investopedia.com/terms/d/dodd-frank-financial-regulatory-reform-bill.asp

52. Macrotrends. Dow Jones—DJIA—100 Year Historical Chart. Interactive chart of the Dow Jones Industrial Average (DJIA) stock market index for the last one hundred years. Historical data is inflation-adjusted using the headline CPI and each data point represents the month-end closing value. The current month is updated on an hourly basis with today's latest value.

https://www.macrotrends.net/1319/dow-jones-100-year-historical-chart

53. Paradigm: Is a widely accepted example, belief, or concept. An example of paradigm is evolution. An example of paradigm is the earth being round.

https://en.wikipedia.org/wiki/Paradigm

54. Full Secular Bull-Bear Cycle: Secular bull market is characterized by above-average stock market returns by the S&P 500 for a long time, typically ten to twenty years. Periodic bear markets spring up within a secular bull market until the next cyclical bull market takes over and carries the market to even higher highs. A cyclical bull market refers to one that lasts a few months to a few years.

- Consistent rise in stock prices
- Healthy economy
- Geographic and political certainty

http://www.wyattresearch.com/markets/bull-markets/

NOTES

55. People by Nature Are Universally Optimistic: Despite calamities from economic recessions, wars, and famine to a flu epidemic afflicting the earth, a new study from the University of Kansas and Gallup indicates that humans are by nature optimistic.

   https://www.sciencedaily.com/releases/2009/05/090524122539. htm

56. Federal Deposit Insurance Corporation (FDIC): Is a US government corporation providing deposit insurance to depositors in US commercial banks and savings institutions. The FDIC was created by the 1933 Banking Act, enacted during the Great Depression to restore trust in the American banking system. More than one-third of banks failed in the years before the FDIC's creation, and bank runs were common. The insurance limit was initially US $2,500 per ownership category, and this was increased several times over the years. Since the passage of the Dodd-Frank Wall Street Reform and Consumer Protection Act in 2011, the FDIC insures deposits in member banks up to US $250,000 per ownership category.

   https://en.wikipedia.org/wiki/Federal_Deposit_Insurance_Corporation

57. AIDS/HIV: The human immunodeficiency virus (HIV) attacks the cells of the immune system, which protects the body from infection. HIV travels through bodily fluids and can be transmitted through unprotected sex, blood transfusions, the sharing of contaminated surgical equipment, pregnancy, childbirth, or breastfeeding. If left untreated, HIV can develop into acquired immunodeficiency syndrome, or AIDS. AIDS refers to the most advanced stages of an HIV infection.

   https://academy4sc.org/video/hiv-aids-act-up/?utm_campaign=&utm_medium=ppc&utm_source=adwords&utm_term=aids&hsa_tgt=kwd-19272081&hsa_mt=b&hsa_acc=2755491261&hsa_grp=139821711980&hsa_ver=3&hsa_src=g&hsa_cam=17795252810&hsa_net=adwords&hsa_kw=aids&hsa_

ad=611107488207&gad_source=1&gclid=EAIaIQobChMI5uK-
-rarhAMVzp9aBR1AugSSEAAYBCAAEgKvwPD_BwE

58. Tobacco-Related Mortality: Overall mortality among both male and female smokers in the United States is about three times higher than that among similar people who never smoked.

    https://archive.cdc.gov/#/details?url=https://www.cdc.gov/tobacco/data_statistics/fact_sheets/health_effects/tobacco_related_mortality/index.htm

59. Laws of Agency: Is an area of commercial law dealing with a set of contractual, quasi-contractual, and non-contractual fiduciary relationships that involve a person, called the agent, that is authorized to act on behalf of another (called the principal) to create legal relations with a third party. Succinctly, it may be referred to as the equal relationship between a principal and an agent whereby the principal, expressly or implicitly, authorizes the agent to work under his or her control and on his or her behalf. The agent is, thus, required to negotiate on behalf of the principal or bring him or her and third parties into contractual relationship. This branch of law separates and regulates the relationships between:

    - Agents and principals (internal relationship), known as the principal-agent relationship;
    - Agents and the third parties with whom they deal on their principals' behalf (external relationship); and
    - Principals and the third parties when the agents deal. https://en.wikipedia.org/wiki/Law_of_agency

60. General Motors Company: Commonly referred to as General Motors (GM), is an American multinational corporation headquartered in Detroit that designs, manufactures, markets, and distributes vehicles and vehicle parts, and sells financial services, with global headquarters in Detroit's Renaissance Center. It was originally founded by William C.

Durant on September 16, 1908, as a holding company. The company is the largest American automobile manufacturer, and one of the world's largest. As of 2018, General Motors is ranked #10 on the Fortune 500 rankings of the largest US corporations by total revenue.

https://en.wikipedia.org/wiki/General_Motors

61. Modern Portfolio Theory: Modern Portfolio Theory, also known as MPT, can help investors choose a set of investments that comprise one portfolio. Together the investment securities combine in such a way as to reduce market risk through diversification while achieving optimal returns. Even if you find that you don't agree with the idea of modern portfolio theory, learning the basics of MPT can help you become a better investor.

https://www.thebalance.com/what-is-mpt-2466539

62. Efficient Frontier: A combination of assets, that is, a portfolio, is referred to as "efficient" if it has the best possible expected level of return for its level of risk (which is represented by the standard deviation of the portfolio's return). Here, every possible combination of risky assets can be plotted in risk-expected return space, and the collection of all such possible portfolios defines a region in this space. In the absence of the opportunity to hold a risk-free asset, this region is the opportunity set (the feasible set). The positively sloped (upward-sloped) top boundary of this region is a portion of a hyperbola and is called the "efficient frontier."

https://en.wikipedia.org/wiki/Efficient_frontier

63. Greg Melia, "The Disease of Ease" Melia Advisory Group: Understands the value of every dollar and how hard people have worked to earn it. Many investors simply suggest "staying the course" at any cost, which has left many hardworking Americans with little to nothing left for retirement. With a thorough understanding of the market cycle, Melia Advisory Group is prepared to properly equip individuals with

investments that PROVIDE INCOME, PROTECT ASSETS, and give PEACE OF MIND.

http://www.meliaadvisorygroup.com/

64. New York Stock Exchange: (NYSE, nicknamed "The Big Board") is an American stock exchange located at 11 Wall Street, Lower Manhattan, New York City, New York. It is by far the world's largest stock exchange by market capitalization of its listed companies at US $30.1 trillion as of February 2018. The average daily trading value was approximately US $169 billion in 2013. The NYSE trading floor is located at 11 Wall Street and is composed of twenty-one rooms used for the facilitation of trading. A fifth trading room, located at 30 Broad Street, was closed in February 2007. The main building and the 11 Wall Street building were designated National Historic Landmarks in 1978.

https://en.wikipedia.org/wiki/New_York_Stock_Exchange

65. Recency Effect: Two traditional classes of theories explain the recency effect, The Dual-Store Model and Single-Store Model.

https://en.wikipedia.org/wiki/Serial-position_effect#Recency_effect

66. Mutual Fund: A mutual fund is a company that pools money from many investors and invests the money in securities such as stocks, bonds, and short-term debt. The combined holdings of the mutual fund are known as its portfolio. Investors buy shares in mutual funds. Each share represents an investor's part ownership in the fund and the income it generates.

https://www.investor.gov/investing-basics/investment-products/mutual-funds

67. Bond Mutual Fund: A mutual fund that generates a minimum return is part of the fixed-income category. A fixed-income mutual fund focuses on investments that pay a set rate of return, such as government bonds, corporate bonds, or other debt instruments. The fund

portfolio generates interest income that is passed on to the shareholders. Sometimes referred to as bond funds, these funds are often actively managed and seek to buy relatively undervalued bonds to sell them at a profit.

https://www.investopedia.com/terms/m/mutualfund.asp

68. Securities and Exchange Commission: The US Securities and Exchange Commission (SEC) is an independent agency of the US federal government. The SEC holds primary responsibility for enforcing the federal securities laws, proposing securities rules, and regulating the securities industry, the nation's stock and options exchanges, and other activities and organizations, including the electronic securities markets in the United States.

https://en.wikipedia.org/wiki/U.S._Securities_and_Exchange_Commission

69. The Bloomberg Terminal: Is a computer software system provided by the financial data vendor Bloomberg L.P. that enables professionals in the financial service sector and other industries to access the Bloomberg Professional service through which users can monitor and analyze real-time financial market data and place trades on the electronic trading platform. The system also provides news, price quotes, and messaging across its proprietary secure network. It is well-known among the financial community for its black interface, which is not optimized for user experience but has become a recognizable trait of the service.

https://en.wikipedia.org/wiki/Bloomberg_Terminal

70. Large-Cap Stocks: A company with a capitalization of more than $10 billion. Market capitalization (market cap) is the market value of a publicly traded company's outstanding shares. Market capitalization is equal to the share price multiplied by the number of shares outstanding. As outstanding stock is bought and sold in public markets, capitaliza-

tion could be used as an indicator of public opinion of a company's net worth and is a determining factor in some forms of stock valuation.

https://en.wikipedia.org/wiki/Market_capitalization

71. US Inflation Rate 1960–1923: Inflation as measured by the consumer price index reflects the annual percentage change in the cost to the average consumer of acquiring a basket of goods and services that may be fixed or changed at specified intervals, such as yearly. The Laspeyres formula is generally used.

https://www.macrotrends.net/countries/USA/united-states/inflation-rate-cpi

72. 2023 US Banking Crisis: Over the course of five days in March 2023, three small- to mid-size US banks failed, triggering a sharp decline in global bank stock prices and swift response by regulators to prevent potential global contagion. Silicon Valley Bank (SVB) failed when a bank run was triggered after it sold its Treasury bond portfolio at a large loss, causing depositor concerns about the bank's liquidity. The bonds had lost significant value as market interest rates rose after the bank had shifted its portfolio to longer-maturity bonds. The bank's clientele was primarily technology companies and wealthy individuals holding large deposits, but balances exceeding $250,000 were not insured by the FDIC.

https://en.wikipedia.org/wiki/2023_United_States_banking_crisis

73. Magnificent 7 Rally Sheds Light on the Need for Capped Indexes: After an abysmal 2022, the technology industry staged a remarkable comeback in the first half of 2023. The tech giants that have become known as "the Magnificent Seven"—Apple, Tesla, Nvidia, Microsoft, Alphabet, Meta, and Amazon—led the rally, considerably outpaced other US large-cap companies, and propelled their already mega market caps to new heights.

https://www.lseg.com/en/insights/ftse-russell/magnificent-seven-rally-sheds-light-need-capped-indexes

74. Gallup Business Journal: Of all the important and interesting findings Dr. Kahneman and Dr. Deaton's research has uncovered, the most reported finding is that people with an annual household income of $75,000 are about as happy as anyone gets. More specifically, those with annual household incomes below $75,000 give lower responses to both life evaluation and emotional well-being questions. But people with an annual household income of more than $75,000 don't have commensurately higher levels of emotional well-being, even though their life evaluation rating continues to increase.

    https://news.gallup.com/businessjournal/150671/happiness-is-love-and-75k.aspx

75. Advisors' Academy: Advisors' Academy was founded in 2007 by David J. Scranton with a vision to recruit other highly successful, motivated advisors and teach them how to achieve even higher levels of success—while always putting the interests of their clients first.

    https://advisorsacademy.com/#about

76. Sound Income Strategies: Sound Income Strategies is a registered investment advisory firm and money manager with more than $2.68 billion of assets under management as of Q1 2024. Sound Income Strategies seeks to help clients achieve their financial goals through actively managed fixed-income strategies designed to protect assets and generate interest and dividends.

    https://soundincomestrategies.com/

77. Jim Beeland Rogers Jr.: Born October 19, 1942, is an American businessman and financial commentator based in Singapore. Rogers is the Chairman of Rogers Holdings and Beeland Interests, Inc. Between January 1, 1999, and January 5, 2002, Rogers did another Guinness World Record journey through 116 countries, covering 245,000 km

with his wife, Paige Parker, in a custom-made Mercedes. The trip began in Iceland, which was about to celebrate the 1000th anniversary of Leif Eriksson's first trip to America. On January 5, 2002, they were back in New York City and their home on Riverside Drive. He wrote *Adventure Capitalist* following this around-the-world adventure. It is currently one of his best-selling books.

https://en.wikipedia.org/wiki/Jim_Rogers

78. Robert Shiller: Born March 29, 1946, is an American economist (Nobel Laureate in 2013), academic, and best-selling author. As of 2018, he serves as a Sterling Professor of Economics at Yale University and is a fellow at the Yale School of Management's International Center for Finance.

   https://en.wikipedia.org/wiki/Robert_J._Shiller

79. Marc Faber: Born February 28, 1946, is a Swiss investor based in Thailand. Faber is publisher of the Gloom Boom & Doom Report newsletter and is the director of Marc Faber Ltd, which acts as an investment advisor and fund manager.

   https://en.wikipedia.org/wiki/Marc_Faber

80. Steve Forbes Jr.: Born July 18, 1947, is an American publishing executive, who was twice a candidate for the nomination of the Republican Party for president of the United States. Forbes is the editor-in-chief of Forbes, a business magazine.

   https://en.wikipedia.org/wiki/Steve_Forbes

81. Peter David Schiff: Born March 23, 1963, is an American stockbroker, financial commentator, and radio personality. He is CEO and chief global strategist of Euro Pacific Capital Inc., a broker-dealer based in Westport, Connecticut.

   https://en.wikipedia.org/wiki/Peter_Schiff

NOTES

82. Dan Gainor: Is the vice president of Business and Culture for the MRC and has been with the organization for more than ten years. He heads up both our MRC Business and MRC Culture departments, including our popular Soros Project. He is a veteran editor with more than three decades of experience in print and online media. Gainor has appeared on Fox News, the Fox Business Network, CNN, CNN HN, CBS, NBC, CNBC, EWTN, The Blaze, and Newsmax TV and has a regular spot on the One America News Network.

    http://archive2.mrc.org/author/dan-gainor

83. George Franklin Gilder: Born November 29, 1939, is an American investor, writer, economist, techno-utopian advocate, and co-founder of the Discovery Institute.

    https://en.wikipedia.org/wiki/George_Gilder

84. Enron Corporation: Was an American energy, commodities, and services company based in Houston, Texas. It was founded in 1985 as a merger between Houston Natural Gas and InterNorth, both relatively small regional companies. Before its bankruptcy on December 3, 2001, Enron employed approximately 29,000 staff and was a major electricity, natural gas, communications, and pulp and paper company, with claimed revenues of nearly $101 billion during 2000. Fortune named Enron "America's Most Innovative Company" for six consecutive years.

    https://en.wikipedia.org/wiki/Enron

85. WorldCom: The WorldCom bankruptcy proceedings were held before US Federal Bankruptcy Judge Arthur J. Gonzalez, who simultaneously heard the Enron bankruptcy proceedings, which were the second largest bankruptcy case resulting from one of the largest corporate fraud scandals. None of the criminal proceedings against WorldCom and its officers and agents were originated by referral from Gonzalez or the Department of Justice lawyers. By the bankruptcy reorganization agreement, the company paid $750 million to the SEC in cash and

stock in the new MCI, which was intended to be paid to wronged investors.

https://en.wikipedia.org/wiki/MCI_Inc.

CHARTS:

Source Chart A (Page 4)—Standard and Poor's 500—Thirteen Years of No Growth:

https://finance.yahoo.com/quote/%5EGSPC?p=^GSPC

2000—The Bubble Bursts: At the turn of the century, the S&P 500 would crack 1,500 for the first time, before embarking on a three-year slide that began with the bursting of the internet bubble and losses of 9 percent for the index for the year as a whole.

https://www.macrotrends.net/2324/sp-500-historical-chart-data

The Great Recession:

No major shifts as far as the top ten are concerned, but 2008 is a year many investors remember well, as the S&P 500 took a nasty tumble. The bellwether index lost more than 36%, as the US financial crisis wreaked havoc on equities across the board. This would, unfortunately, only be the beginning of global economic woes, which spread to other areas of the world in the coming months and years.

https://www.macrotrends.net/2324/sp-500-historical-chart-data

Source Chart B (Page 7)—Life expectancy in the United States, 1860–2020:

Over the past 160 years, life expectancy (from birth) in the United States has risen from 39.4 years in 1860, to 78.9 years in 2020. One of the major reasons for the overall increase of life expectancy in the

NOTES

last two centuries is the fact that the infant and child mortality rates have decreased by so much during this time. Medical advancements, fewer wars, and improved living standards also mean that people are living longer than they did in previous centuries.

Published by Aaron O'Neill, Jun 21, 2022

https://www.statista.com/statistics/1040079/life-expectancy-united-states-all-time/

Source Chart C (Page 11)—Dow Jones Industrial Average—1982–2000:

Data is available from July 2, 1982, DJIA of 797.00 points to January 3, 2000, DJIA of 11,522.56 points and suggests a growth of about fourteen times. From Data supplied by Samuel H. Williamson, "Daily Closing Value of the Dow Jones Average, 1885 to Present," MeasuringWorth, 2015.

https://www.macrotrends.net/1319/dow-jones-100-year-historical-chart

Source Chart D (Page 66)—S&P 500 Secular Bear Market—1966–1982:

Data is available from January 1, 1966, S&P 500 of 93.32 points to S&P 500 December 1, 1982, of 139.40 points. Showing bull and bear markets.

https://www.macrotrends.net/2324/sp-500-historical-chart-data

Source Chart E (Page 71)—US 10-Year Treasury Bond Rate 1964-2024:

As Robert Shiller's new 2009 preface to his prescient classic on behavioral economics and market volatility asserts, the irrational exuberance of the stock and housing markets "has been ended by an economic crisis of a magnitude not seen since the Great Depression of the 1930s."

- US Treasury for recent 10-Year Treasury Rates.

183

- Robert Shiller and his book Irrational Exuberance for long-term historic 10-Year Treasury Yields.

https://www.macrotrends.net

Source Chart F (Page 77)—Federal Reserve Balance Sheet 2007–2024:

Since the beginning of the financial market turmoil in August 2007, the Federal Reserve's balance sheet has grown in size and has changed in composition. Total assets of the Federal Reserve have increased significantly from $870 billion on August 8, 2007, to $4.5 trillion on January 14, 2015, and have been declining since the beginning of the FOMC's balance sheet normalization program in October 2017.

https://www.statista.com

Source Chart G (Page 81)—S&P 500 Share Buybacks:

The amount of shares repurchased by S&P 500 companies in the last three months of 2018 hit a record, marking the fourth consecutive quarterly all-time high and the longest such streak since S&P Dow Jones Indices began tracking repurchases two decades ago. Source: FactSet Fundamentals. https://www. marketwatch.com/story/stock-buybacks-among-sp-500-companies-mark-a-record-streak-2019-03-25

Source Data:

https://www.google.com/search?rlz=1C1CHBF_ enUS801US801&biw=1920&bih=920&tbm=isch&sa=1&ei= Dq_IXIyI4zisAX lzob4Bg&q=s%26p+500+share+buybacks++ factset+fundamentals&oq=s%26p+500+share+buybacks++ factset+fundamentals&gs_l=img.3...68939.68939..69182   0.0..0.114.114.0j1......0....1.. gws-wiz-img.3Q0eOHUxqy4#imgrc= 6r7_mqZvlmckLM:

Source Chart H (Page 136)—Returns of S&P 500 Index Stocks by Dividend Policy: Growth of $100 (1973-2022):

Source: Ned Davis Research and Hartford Funds, 2/22.

NOTES

TABLES:

Table A (Page 63)—Source—The Expansion of the US Stock Market, 1885–1930: Historical Facts and Theoretical Fashions:

https://www.jstor.org/stable/23700715?seq=1#page_scan_tab_contents

Table B (Page 121)—Source—Fixed-Income Investing, Mutual Funds:

Bond mutual funds are mutual funds that invest in bonds. Like other mutual funds, bond mutual funds are like baskets that hold dozens or hundreds of individual securities (in this case, bonds). A bond fund manager or team of managers will research the fixed-income markets for the best bonds based upon the overall objective of the bond mutual fund. The manager(s) will then purchase and sell bonds based upon economic and market activity. Managers also have to sell funds to meet redemptions (withdrawals) of investors.

https://www.thebalance.com/bonds-vs-bond-funds-2466790

Milton Keynes UK
Ingram Content Group UK Ltd.
UKHW011449300624
444949UK00010B/65